102 WAYS TO WRITE A NOVEL

102 WAYS
TO WRITE A NOVEL

Indispensable Tips for the Writer of Fiction

ALEX QUICK

First published in 2012 by Old Street Publishing Ltd,
Trebinshun House, Brecon LD3 7PX
www.oldstreetpublishing.co.uk

ISBN 978 1 906964 92 4

10 9 8 7 6 5 4 3 2 1

A CIP catalogue record for this title is available from the British Library.

Printed and bound in Great Britain

To Graham Rider

CONTENTS

Building Plot

The matter of structure

Types of prose writing

Point of View

Language

INTRODUCTION

This book emerged from several years' teaching Adult Education courses in novel-writing. My students worked hard, asked good questions and excited my literary envy. I certainly learned more from teaching them than they did from being taught.

There are several ways you could organize a book called '102 Ways to Write a Novel'. For example you could do it by making a list entirely of practical methods, such as: 'Way No. 1: write sitting under a tree; Way No. 2: write entirely using snippets cut out from leader articles in the *Daily Telegraph*', etc. However, in this book, the 'ways' are ways of thinking, approaches to writing a novel, matters that writers can profitably chew over. I hope it forms a mini-curriculum for aspiring novelists.

For those who wish to study further, a bibliography is given at the back. But the real education, of course, is the practice of writing itself.

Alex Quick, Norwich, 2012

BEFORE YOU START

1.

CONSIDER YOUR MOTIVES

Why do you want to write a novel?

> To show that you can do it?
> To score off your old English teacher?
> To earn money?
> To be recognised in the street?
> To attract literary groupies?
> To tell a particular story?
> To move people?
> Because you have to?

The last is probably the best reason. You will need a lot of stamina to write a novel. If you absolutely must write one, then it might actually get written.

The other reasons are not bad either. It is perfectly fine to write a novel in the hope of scoring off an old English teacher, or attracting literary groupies. If these reasons are strong enough, they will keep you writing, keep you exploring, and may finally engender a novel. Whether that novel is ever published is, of course, another matter;

and whether, once it is published, it satisfies those initial desires, is another matter again.

The important thing is to be honest with yourself about why you are writing. If your motives are ignoble, examine them and see if you can live with them. Buried shame is not a good companion at the beginning of a writing project.

If your motives are pure and clean, good for you. Now you know why you are doing what you are doing, and can proceed with God and St Cassian of Imola on your side.

St Cassian of Imola is very dear to writers: he was stabbed to death by the iron pens of his students.

2.

THINK ABOUT WHAT SORT OF NOVEL YOU WANT TO WRITE

The term 'novel' is a broad one. Let's take considerations of length first. A work of fiction that lays claim to being a novel should be 50,000 words long (which comes to around 150 pages in a standard paperback) or more.

Anything under that, and the novel acquires a suffix and becomes a novella. But there is no upper limit to a novel's length. Meganovels of a million words or more have been written and published. The exigencies of modern publishing usually demand single volumes, but in previous centuries novels would often be published in multiple volumes ('three-deckers' or more).

Then there is the question of form. Some novels are 'loose baggy monsters' (in Henry James' phrase) which ramble from one incident to another, and appear, on the surface at least, to have little structure. *Women* by Charles Bukowski is an example. Some novels are presented in the form of diaries or as letters. Others are written entirely in dialogue (anything by Ivy Compton-Burnett). Yet others (such as *The Inimitable Jeeves* by PG Wodehouse) are essentially composed of linked short stories with an overarching narrative.

Then there is point of view (see section 69 onwards). Your novel can be told from the first, second or third person point of view, with various refinements of each. Even the first person plural is possible. *Then We Came to the End* by Joshua Ferris, about a group of office workers, is composed entirely using 'we' as the subject.

Then there is time and setting. Do you want to write a family saga beginning in the Middle Ages and extending to the present day? Do you want to write a misery memoir set in Indo-Catholic Sweden?

Before you start, the possibilities are truly huge. The best thing to do is to decide on something that feels intuitively right for you, rather than lumbering yourself with something which you feel you ought to do, but which fails to grab you.

But when you do choose something, you need to be prepared to stick with it, for better or for worse, for richer for poorer, for as long as ye both can stand the sight of one another. As in a marriage, the key word is commitment. There will be highs and lows. Some of the time it will be exhilarating, but the rest of the time it will be very hard work.

3.
HOW FAR SHOULD YOU WRITE FOR A MARKET?

As well as the above considerations (length, form, point of view, time and setting), there is also the question of who your novel is for. You may wish to consider writing for a particular group of readers.

In the last twenty years there has been a huge growth in the publication of novels for young adults – many, but not all, featuring the undead. There is a big market in novels for children. There are novels chiefly for women (romance, 'chick-lit') and for men (action thrillers, adventure novels). It may also be worth bearing in mind that most novels are bought by women – though they may be buying them, in many cases, for men.

Then there is the distinction between 'literary fiction' and 'genre fiction'. Literary fiction is the 'highbrow' version of the novel and will often tend to concentrate on the inner lives of characters, feature complex and poeticized modes of expression or be structurally experimental. Anything by Jeanette Winterson or Salman Rushdie would qualify. Genre fiction, on the other hand, is the type of thing you find at airports (we call it airport fiction, the French call it *littérature de gare*), which concentrates on telling a rattling good yarn. The main genres include the crime novel, the thriller, the romance novel and the sci-fi novel. In reality there is a lot of overlap between literary and genre fiction – literary fiction will often feature hectic plots, and genre fiction may contain exquisitely developed characters – and few authors like being pigeonholed in either category.

There's nothing wrong in writing for a market. Thousands of authors successfully do just that every year. There is something wrong in insincerely writing for a market. If you don't love your genre or niche, and are writing just to hoodwink the public and make money, you will almost certainly be unsuccessful. Genre writers love their genres. They work within them to produce works of art that they consider emotionally engaging, subtle and beautiful.

It is often a good idea to have a particular reader or group of readers in mind. Some people keep in mind a single trusted friend. If you do this, then you are, in a sense, writing for a market, even if only a market of one. It's a very common strategy – and it's nothing to be ashamed of.

4.
THINK ABOUT THE ROLE
OF THE STORYTELLER

There's something about storytelling that is very trivial
when it comes down to it. Writing a novel, which is
basically a load of lies, is a rather odd thing to do, when
the other things in life – birth, death, conflict, suffering –
are so urgent and so terrible. What is the point of making
stuff up when real life gives us so much to deal with and to
bear, and regularly outdoes anything fiction can produce?

However, there is another way of looking at this. As
human beings, we have an insatiable thirst for stories,
whether they be on television, in books, in cinemas,
or in churches. We swim in them all day long. If you
think about your basic needs, you will put some sort of
entertainment high on the list. A recent government
report said that any family without a television – and a
rather nice one, with lots of channels and satellite access –
could be counted as living in poverty.

At the cave mouth, after the unsuccessful hunt, we
needed someone to explain things, to give us dignity
in the face of loss, to keep us going. We needed

someone to explain what the births, deaths, conflicts and suffering were actually about. These explanations were so important that they could literally make the difference between life and death, between wanting to go on and wanting to give up.

Stories shape how we look at the world. Successful story-creators are extremely powerful people who are guaranteed a job for life.

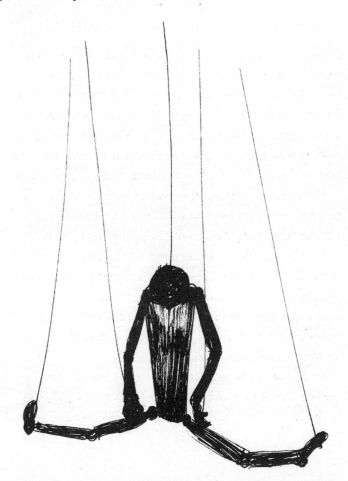

5.
CAN WRITING BE TAUGHT?

The answer is a qualified yes. It is also a qualified no.

Someone who wishes to learn to write a novel has four main resources: books about writing, novels themselves, human teachers, and writing itself. Let's take these in order.

Books about writing are there to teach the craft. They can tell you what a metaphor is, how to punctuate, what makes effective dialogue, and how to create suspense. They give you the techniques to do the job and to criticize what you have written. (This last is very important. Ernest Hemingway said that 'the only writers are re-writers'; much of your effort as a writer will be directed towards revising what you have already done.)

The second resource is books, novels, themselves. When Penelope Lively was a girl, her governess wrote to Somerset Maugham for advice. Penelope wanted to be a writer: what should she do? Maugham wrote back: 'She should read.' Later in life Penelope recognized the excellence of this advice. A writer must read, because a writer must know about literature. More than that, a writer must love literature. Large loves and large hatreds – these are essential to any writer.

Human teachers are also useful at a certain stage in a writer's development. A fledgling writer can look at an established writer and think: 'Do I really want to spend my life worrying over sentences? Do I want to be like this person? Do I want to be an observer, on the margin of life, or do I want to be a doer?' A teacher will show you an example of a person who is serious about writing. That vision may inspire you – or it may put you off. Both services are valuable.

The final resource is the practice of writing itself. This trumps all the others. After a lot of practice, you get an ear for what works on the page and what doesn't. You develop a sense of rhythm (Virginia Woolf said that literary style is all about rhythm). You discover your personality in words. That is what I meant when I said that the answer to the question 'Can writing be taught?' is a qualified no. The first three techniques are insufficient on their own. Writing, in the end, cannot be taught – unless you teach yourself.

PRACTICAL CONSIDERATIONS

6.
MAKE TIME AND SPACE FOR WRITING

Writing a novel, in almost all cases, is about the slow accumulation of words over a long period of time. There are exceptions to this: Samuel Johnson wrote *Rasselas* in two weeks. But for most of us, a novel is a slog.

Added to this, you will almost always wish to re-write what you have written. You will probably have to write your book all the way through more than once. Barbara Kingsolver (author of *The Poisonwood Bible*) says that she usually finds herself writing a novel-sized introduction to her novel before she begins writing her novel.

Your novel may take many months or years, conceivably decades, to finish. And it will have to be done bit by bit. You will need to work at it regularly, solidly, determinedly, day after day after day, like a prisoner tunnelling through the wall with a bar of soap.

With this in mind you need to give yourself some room. Firstly, identify the time that you can devote to writing. Most British adults watch three hours of television a day. Try cutting that out. Do you have a long commute? Think about what you could do with that, and a notebook. How about weekends? Is there any free space there? Write a timetable in which you identify a block of time every day – or if not every day, then as many days in the week as you can. You can vary the times of day that you write, though personally I think it is best to keep to a single time.

Similarly with space. Find a place in the house which is as far as possible from distractions. Don't try and work in the living room with the television on. Work in the children's bedrooms if necessary, while they are watching TV downstairs. Install a writer's shed like the one Roald Dahl worked in.

In Louise Doughty's excellent book *A Novel in a Year* she recommends an exercise called 'Allies and Enemies'. This consists in identifying the things that help you write and those that hinder you. Typical Allies might include quiet, a good word processor, the encouragement of friends and family, and Lemsip (if you are Andrew Motion). Typical Enemies might include the TV, radio, phone, cooking, email, the internet, and the need to earn money.

Writing is hard because you will never be paid by the hour. All your time and effort may be completely wasted. You've got to do it because it is part of you and because you feel excited by it.

7.

WRITE IN THE MORNINGS?

It seems that the majority of professional writers write in the mornings.

> I always write in the morning. In the morning one's head is particularly fresh. (Leo Tolstoy)

> First coffee. Then a bowel movement. Then the muse joins me. (Gore Vidal)

> I prefer to get up very early in the morning and work. I don't want to speak to anybody or see anybody. Perfect silence. I work until the vein is out. (Katherine Anne Porter)

> I generally go to work right after breakfast. I sit right down to the machine. If I find I'm not able to write, I quit. (Ernest Hemingway)

> I work mornings only. I go out to lunch. Afternoons I play with the baby, walk with my husband, or shovel mail. (Annie Dillard)

The reason, I would guess, is psychological: writing requires courage and application, and there is no guarantee of any reward at the end of it. Most writers want to get it over with. They know they've got to do it (otherwise they wouldn't be writers), and they know that once they've done it they are going to feel pretty fantastic, but actually getting down to it is difficult, and the longer they put it off the more nervous, irritable, depressed and frankly despairing they will be. They know that whatever they accomplish that morning will be just one crampon driven into the novel-mountain – but they know that novel-mountains are only climbed one crampon at a time. So they do this difficult, possibly dangerous and futile thing as early as possible, before their nerve fails them. Only afterwards can they relax and become human beings. Try interrupting a novelist around 10am and you'll see what I mean.

However, non-professional writers, and those who are not unemployed or retired, will probably find it hard to work in the mornings à la Tolstoy. Why? Because they will need to earn money to feed themselves.

95% of novelists – and here I'm speaking about those who actually publish novels – have other jobs. Being a novelist, except in that rare 5% of cases, does not pay enough to support the average person, let alone the average family.

So work in the mornings if you can. But if, like most people, you need to earn a living, you may find it necessary to make different arrangements.

8.
DECIDE ON A WORD-COUNT

If you can't write in the mornings and your time is fractured during the week, another solution might be to decide on a daily or weekly word-count.

In this way you work not so much with blocks of time but with blocks of words. You work an hour here, a half-hour there – whenever you can find the time – until you have the requisite number. If you reach the weekend and you still haven't managed to achieve your weekly word-count, you know it will be a busy literary weekend. If you've accumulated enough words in the week, you know you can get on with something less important, such as repairing the hole in the roof.

In reality, most writers will employ some combination of the two methods. They will sit down at a particular time of the day and stay there until the word-count has clocked up. On some days this will take forever, and on other days it will all be done in one ecstatic deluge.

What is a good figure for a day or week? There's no correct answer. It will depend on what you can realistically expect, given the other conditions of your life. Some write just 500 words per day. Others write thousands. Some, like Oscar Wilde, write a single perfect word in the morning and cross it out in the evening.

A good figure for a full working day, with no other distractions, might be something like a thousand words. At this rate, working seven days a week, you could complete a novel of 90,000 words in three months. However, such a rapid pace would take no account of revision. You might delete most or all of those thousand words the next day, taking you only a little further forward in word-count terms (though you might make a lot of progress in knowing exactly where it is you don't want to go with your novel). And so it would proceed, in a series of jumps forward and back. Writing the novel in this way might therefore take six months rather than three. Of course, this would represent only the creation of the first 90,000-word draft. Now the final revision would begin (see section 91 onwards), which might take another six months – or longer.

All writers are different. You need to experiment to find something that suits your own personal rhythm, and then stick to it.

[398 words]

9.

KEEP A COMMONPLACE BOOK

A writer may be defined as a person who always carries a pen. As definitions go, it isn't a bad one. A writer is a person who thinks about, and practises, writing; and as a practitioner they will wish, at any moment, to make notes.

Along with the pen goes some sort of paper. The inconvenience of scribbling on discarded envelopes means that a notebook, or 'commonplace book' is sooner or later called for. 'Commonplace book' is a somewhat archaic term, but it's descriptive: it is for things, often commonplace, that can later be used in your writing. It might contain:

- ideas for plots, subplots, themes and characters;
- descriptions of people, places, buildings, natural objects,
activities;
- lists of possible names of characters, places and things;
- metaphors, imagery;
- scraps of dialogue, overheard conversation, slang words,

words in foreign languages, definitions, reflections on language in general;
• quotations, inspirational or otherwise;
• drawings of things (a good way to keep records, especially if annotated);
• reactions to films, art, books or music;
• title ideas;
• specific descriptions of things from a sensory point of view (see section 87 onwards), which may merit a commonplace book all their own, with relevant sections for each of the senses: sight, hearing, smell, sound and taste.

Literally anything can go into the commonplace book, whether or not it is immediately relevant to the novel. The commonplace book is partly there just to keep you in the habit of writing, to flex the writing muscle (which definitely exists). Sometimes you will look at an old commonplace book and think: 'what the hell is that doing there? I don't even remember writing that.' It's actually there because it enabled you to think about writing, and to write, at that moment – and thinking about, and practising writing, is what a writer does.

Some may find the commonplace book a little old-fashioned. But if the alternative is getting out a small computer, powering it up, finding a file, adding to it and saving it, I would rather have a notebook. Notebooks are cheap and portable, and can be used in the bath, standing up on a crowded train or in a gale at the top of the Eiffel Tower.

10.
COMPUTERS OR PAPER?

For the main business of writing the novel (as opposed
to taking notes in the field – see the previous section),
the vast majority of novelists nowadays will use a word-
processor. It's easy to see why. A word-processor makes it
easy to print copies, to count words, and to edit and revise.
Revision in the days of longhand writing or typing must
have been nightmarish. Sofia Tolstoy copied out *War and
Peace* for Leo eight times.

Plus the fact that there is no spellcheck in a pencil.

Having said that, there are still some people who feel
that word-processors tend to homogenize literary culture.
Vladimir Nabokov composed his novels on small index cards:
his prose would almost certainly have been different if he'd
used a computer. Other writers had other quirky methods
– Dick Francis wrote in children's exercise books, Truman
Capote prone on a sofa – all of them giving subtle flavours to
their writing. Now most of these quirky methods are gone.

Some even feel the typewriter was a mistake. Edmund
Wilson said: 'I believe that the typewriter has probably done
more than anything else to deteriorate English prose.'

Perhaps the greatest problem is the word-processor's proximity to the internet. If anything tends to homogenize prose (or, at least, ideas), it's the internet. If two writers in different parts of Cardiff on the same day both want a picture of Karachi, it's likely now that they'll end up with the same one. This can't be good for fiction.

11.
JOIN A WRITERS' GROUP

It has been said that in any large city, at any time, there is a writer only four feet away. Or is it a rat?

The point is that that there's no need to work in isolation if you don't want to. All sorts of groups exist to give succour to writers.

The most traditional kind is the writers' circle, in which writers get together, perhaps in a rented hall or in members' homes, and discuss each other's writing. Members take it in turn to submit work, which can be circulated in advance (now usually by email). These sessions can be extremely helpful: constructive feedback is always to be welcomed (see section 94), even if you don't agree with it. And you get to meet like-minded people.

Another kind of writer's group is the 'open mic'-style performance group, of which there are now considerably more than in the past. These give you an opportunity to read your work out loud for a limited (maybe five-minute) slot in front of other writers and the general public. They are often more for poets than novelists, though novelists are usually welcome. The experience is invaluable: again, you get instant feedback and meet other writers. You don't need to read if you don't want to, and there's plenty of literary discussion going on. Other, 'salon'-style events will have guest speakers and readers, and perhaps also an 'open-mic' element.

An even newer development is the online writers' group. With an online group, you can sign up and post your work on the internet, where it can be assessed by other writers. There is sometimes a membership fee to be paid, but this is likely to be nominal and is intended merely to discourage the non-serious. Access to the site is then password-protected. With some online groups, you are expected to submit a number of reviews before you are allowed to post work. There are groups for the totality of genres: crime, romance, historical, teen, sci-fi, fantasy, and so on. 'Sharing' through Facebook or email is possible. Some online writers' groups feature contests with cash prizes. On one popular website, the submissions are rated according to a points system, and the top ten novels are read by a representative of Harper Collins!

And if you're really stuck for a writing group, and can't find any online, why not try starting one yourself?

12.
CONSIDER COLLABORATIVE WRITING

After writers' groups, perhaps the next logical step is some kind of collaborative writing.

This might immediately strike you as abhorrent. Writing is something you do alone, surely – like being born, dying or washing under your arms.

However, there are a number of ways to collaborate. Not all involve giving someone else total power over your work. Here are a few of the more mainstream types of collaboration:

• *The Research and Development Model.* In this model, one partner does the background research and the other develops it into fiction. Many writers have had research assistants, from Alexandre Dumas to Dick Francis.
• *The Husband and Wife Model.* This might refer to any partnership, but it is striking that a number of successful ones are married couples. Michael Jacobs and Daniela De Gregorio, for example, write historical crime fiction under the name Michael Gregorio; Nicci Gerrard and Sean French write psychological thrillers

under the name Nicci French. The working methods of such teams may differ widely: in some cases, one partner may write descriptions and the other psychological treatments; and so on.

• *The James Patterson Model.* James Patterson, the crime, thriller, romance and children's writer, works with a number of collaborators in a 'fiction factory', enabling him to publish several books a year. Usually the collaborator writes the first draft and Patterson puts the finishing touches to it. Nice work if you can get it.

• *The Alternating Chapters Model.* In 1969 a literary sensation broke over the heads of an astonished American public: *Naked Came the Stranger, a novel of vice in Long Island.* It later emerged that it had been written by 24 Newsday journalists who had become irritated by the success of soft-porn pulp novels and thought to themselves: 'How hard can this be?' Each journalist wrote one chapter. The results often had to be edited because they were 'too well written'.

• *The Translation Model.* Here, one partner prepares a rough draft from another language and the other works it up into acceptable prose.

... and there are other combinations. Given that writers, historically, have often collaborated (including, of course, Shakespeare), refusal to countenance any interference with one's prose starts looking a little precious.

THE RESEARCH PHASE

13.

ANSWER THE QUESTION: 'WHAT'S YOUR NOVEL ABOUT?'

Most writers go through a research phase before writing a novel. This might involve reading about a place, topic, person, time or historical event. It might involve going to a place or doing some of the things your characters are likely to do.

However, it might be useful first of all to think about your novel in broader terms, and to answer three questions:

- What is your novel's basic plot outline (what's your novel about)?
- What is the subject of your novel?
- What is your novel saying (what's its theme)?

These questions are subtly different and lead to different answers, each of which will provide a mini-summary of your novel-to-be.

The first question is the one novelists get asked at parties: 'What's your novel about?' It's a reasonable question. A good novel is usually identifiably about something. The answer is always going to be reductive, since a sentence is shorter than a novel. But it doesn't mean the question is silly in the first place.

When people ask: 'What's your novel about?' they are asking essentially for a plot outline. In other words, they are really asking: 'What happens in your novel?' If you just say: 'My novel is about love', they will think to themselves: 'Yes, but what's it about?'

Your novel's plot outline is like a movie pitch. It's the essentials of the story, boiled down. 'My novel is about a woman who wakes up in a shipping container and doesn't know how she got there' is close to the kind of thing you should aim for. Something punchy that will both enthuse others and energize your own writing. That's the real value of the exercise. Once you've road-tested your plot outline and got it right, you can refer back to it and check you're still in a position to generate the same levels of interest and excitement.

Plotting is a whole area in itself and there is a part later on in this book devoted specifically to it (section 37 onwards). But the plot outline will probably come to you all at once, as an idea: What if the internet stopped working? What if a teenager became prime minister? What if a man found out he was not related to his father or his son? Worlds turn on such ideas.

14.
DISCOVER YOUR SUBJECT

Now we know what your novel's about. It's about a woman who wakes up in a shipping container and doesn't know how she got there. But what's it about on a deeper level? What is its subject? Is it, perhaps, memory, or endurance?

Your subject is the second on the list of questions mentioned above (i.e. what's it about, what's its subject, and what's it saying). The subject is what lies behind the outline, and what was unsatisfactory at the party. As mentioned before, if someone at a party said to you: 'What's your novel about?' and you replied: 'Love', they'd probably want more information; yet at its core the book would still be about this one thing, love. And it's useful for you at least to know what that thing is.

A subject will often be expressible in one abstract noun: injustice, ambition, sex, revenge, self-sacrifice, endurance, redemption, betrayal (or possibly two words: racial prejudice, corporate greed, family breakdown). It's possible for an author to write several novels, all of which seem different, but which actually have the same subject.

And books by different authors that seem very dissimilar might share a subject. One might argue that the subject of Aldous Huxley's *Brave New World* is liberty, but liberty might also be considered the subject of Jack London's *Call of the Wild*.

How do you discover a subject? Well, that really has to flow from the core of you as a person. If you have been personally involved in some injustice, you may wish to explore how injustice can be perpetrated. If you have ever been in love, you may wish to explore love. A novel is sometimes like an exorcism, sometimes like therapy, sometimes like a self-induced hallucination. It flows ultimately from very personal concerns.

15.
FIND A THEME

The theme is the third way you can sum up your novel (to recap, the first two are outlining the plot and identifying the subject).

A theme is present in a novel if the author has taken the time to ask himself or herself: 'what is my book saying?'

Unlike 'what's your book about?', no one will ever ask you 'what's your book saying?' at parties. It would seem vaguely rude. But it may be important for you to have an answer to it, if only in your own mind. It really goes back to why you wanted to write the book in the first place.

You probably chose your theme at around the same time as you chose your subject. If your subject is 'war', for example, your theme might be 'war is the engine of history' or 'war is hell.' You'll notice that the theme, unlike the subject or the plot outline, has a declarative or polemical tone to it. It makes a concise assertion. Examples of oft-encountered themes are: the love of money is the root of all evil; there's no fool like an old fool; even the most unpromising of people can change; the pen is mightier than the sword; love is a dangerous game; blood is thicker than water; people have strengths they don't know about until they are tested. The theme is the thing that you are saying about the subject. It will be something you feel deeply about and want to demonstrate. It doesn't matter if your theme is unoriginal. To say that love is a dangerous game is no news to anyone. It is your particular take on the theme that will make the words jump off the page.

A theme will probably gain in strength if it is controversial or debatable. Debatability of theme helps your novel to resonate after the novel is over.

A strong theme will also tend to be implicit rather than explicit. In *Lord of the Flies* the theme is something such as 'people revert quickly to savagery' – but it isn't ever stated as such, only implied. As a theme, it is also, you'll notice, debatable.

It's possible to write a novel with no theme, no polemic, no assertion, which still leaves the reader satisfied; but such books will tend to be in the 'slice-of-life' camp. It's also possible to write a book in which the theme is too dominant, too wearyingly insisted-upon. Most writers will try to pitch it somewhere between the two.

16.
VISIT THE LIBRARY

So far I've encouraged you to write about something that flows from the core of yourself as a person, or something that you feel strongly about and want to assert.

Does this mean you can simply sit at home and write out of yourself, as a person, without doing any further investigation into the external world? Not necessarily. There may be characters and scenes in your novel that are remote from your everyday experiences. Research may therefore be called for.

Research usually starts with reading. It's a good idea, if you can, to buy a good selection of volumes on any subject you want to write about, so that you always have them with you and you feel you 'own' the subject. Make notes on what you read, always with an eye to plot or character possibilities. Try not to rely too much on the internet for your reading. Everyone has a computer, and everyone can surf where you surf – but no one in the last twenty years may have held the book you are holding.

If your novel is about a particular historical period, visit museums and archives with collections relating to your period. Find out what people wore, how they spoke, what their houses looked like, what they used for money, what they ate for breakfast, lunch and dinner (and what they called those meals). Handle the letters they wrote, read the newspapers and magazines they read. If your novel concerns recent history, interview those who were around at the time. Or if your novel concerns a particular subject area, interview experts in that area. If your hero is a chemist, interview a chemist. Draw him out and you will understand why for some people chemistry is a passion to rival opera or snowboarding.

Soon it may become necessary to do something more adventurous. If your novel is set in a particular place, go to that place, even if it involves some effort and expense. If your novel is set in China, go to China. (Of course, you might want to avoid giving yourself that particular headache by setting your novel in Hull.)

When you have finished, you will be top-heavy with information. Now, of course, you must use it. But beware of using too much of it. This is the danger of exposition (see section 58). Just because your character plays baseball, it doesn't mean that his speech must be larded with baseball terms.

Research is like nutmeg: a sprinkling of it is marvellous, but in large amounts it ruins the pudding.

17.
ACCUMULATE SPECIFIC DETAIL

As you do your research, your main activity will be the accumulation of detail.

On your trip to China, it will be a waste of time if you just hang around absorbing the atmosphere. You will need actively to gather the type of detail that will convince your readers that the China of your novel is the real China, and not something you've cobbled together from TV programmes and magazines. What sort of ornaments are in ordinary Chinese houses? What sports do people play? How do spectators behave at the matches? Do Chinese cars have bumper stickers? What do they say? What sort of music is played on the radio?

A well-chosen detail gives depth to a character or setting. Many of the best details will be specific and unusual. If you are describing a garage, no one will be surprised to hear it has oil stains on the floor. However they may be surprised and interested if you say that there is a full-size medical skeleton in one corner. Details may also bring a jolt of recognition. When people first move into a house, they often play their stereo extra loud on the first night. Why is that? Left-handed people often use their right hand to move a computer mouse. Why? An author who has taken the time to observe such things and note them down will bring that jolt of recognition from readers who may have noticed them too, but not consciously registered the fact.

You don't have to cram these sorts of details onto every page. Detailed description is rather like metaphor: a little goes a long way. In fact, in bulk, detail can sometimes seem like a cheap attempt to illuminate character. If you introduce a character by saying that she is wearing a cream Marks and Spencer trouser-suit with matching accessories and driving a new Kia Sportage 2 Eco 1.7 CRDi, the reader might not feel you are getting them very far. They would prefer to hear what makes this woman different from every other cream-trouser-suit-wearing Sportage-driving woman in the world. If there is a chocolate stain she hasn't noticed on the lapel of the jacket, you needn't mention it was from Marks and Spencer. If she's left a library book entitled *The Diagnosis and Treatment of Schizophrenia* on top of the Sportage and driven away with it still there, you needn't mention the make of the car.

As with all research, you may not use everything you observe and note down. But your commonplace book (see section 9) should be packed with these kinds of specific details. Re-reading them can be a potent cure for writer's block.

18.
DEFEAT WRITER'S BLOCK

It may be that no amount of time or space, no writer's group, no collaborator, no amount of research, no knowledge of one's subject, plot outline or theme, no help from teachers or self-help guides, and no reading of other novels makes any difference: you simply can't write.

This is writer's block, and it may have many causes. One of the most common is psychological. It often affects beginners. Beginning writers often feel that whatever they write isn't good enough. They feel inadequate.

The dirty little secret however is that nearly all writers feel inadequate. Hemingway said: 'The first draft of anything is shit'; Philip Roth said: 'What you develop is... patience with your own crap, really.' Writers, even those with several novels behind them, often feel doubtful that they can produce another one, and even wonder vaguely how they wrote the others. They are beset by jealousies for other writers who seem to knock them out with gay abandon.

But the trick, as Hemingway and Roth imply, is just to write: write whatever comes into your head, no matter how 'crap'. After a while there will be something there to build on. Eventually something will lead you off in an exciting direction. Writing is the exercise of a muscle that gets more supple the more it is used.

Bearing this in mind – that writing begets writing – another method of defeating writer's block is to write something that isn't your novel. Try, for example, alternating non-fiction and fiction writing. Or, if you don't have any non-fiction projects to hand, try writing a diary, or a blog, or a letter to a friend. These may well suggest something that will have you running back to the novel.

Another method is to do something entirely unrelated. You can play a sport, or do some gardening, or do anything physical. This allows the conscious mind to rest and the subconscious to take over. When you return to your desk you may find that the problems you were experiencing seem less intractable.

Or, if you're already some way through your novel and it has a stalled feel to it, try changing some fundamental aspect of it. Change your main character's name, for example, or their sex, or their location.

Or try writing your book non-chronologically. If you're stuck at a particular place, zip forwards to the next scene that really interests you. In fact, there's no need to write those intervening scenes if they're not interesting. Just leave them out. What was it Elmore Leonard said? 'Leave out the parts that readers tend to skip.'

19.

MAP YOUR MIND

If none of this is working, you may be seriously stalled. This might be the time to try a mindmap.

Mindmapping is a technique that combines elements of free association and chance to pull ideas out of your mind. Variants of it are called clustering, branching or spider drawing, but they're all basically the same.

Start by writing the word 'novel' in the centre of a large sheet of paper. Put the title of the novel underneath, if you have one. Then draw off lines from the centre and at the ends of the lines put words such as 'plot', 'characters', 'location', 'time frame', 'symbolism', 'emotions', 'suspense', 'point of view', 'other media', 'theme', 'genre', or 'conflicts'. Then take each one and elaborate it as per the drawing, radiating out all your notions. Do it quickly, without thinking a great deal. When you've finished, take the ideas that appeal to you most and put a mark by them. Link them up. Now take this circle as something to build on, and write up a plot summary. It's quite possible, using this method, to start with absolutely nothing, and within ten minutes end up with a whole novel (for example, a first person narrative set in the present day, with an antagonist, written in the form of letters, by a dog, featuring a journey, and the sun/moon as a symbol of freedom). If it's a scene you're stuck with, substitute the word 'novel' with the word 'scene', and repeat the same process.

20.
GO!

The ground-work has been laid. The research has been done. The word-processor is exhaling. The timetable has been written out in coloured inks and has been nailed to the wall above your desk. So has your most recent mindmap.

It's time to begin. Start in the middle if you wish, start at the end, even (daring suggestion) start at the beginning, but above and beyond all else, start.

To be a writer one must write.

Avanti!

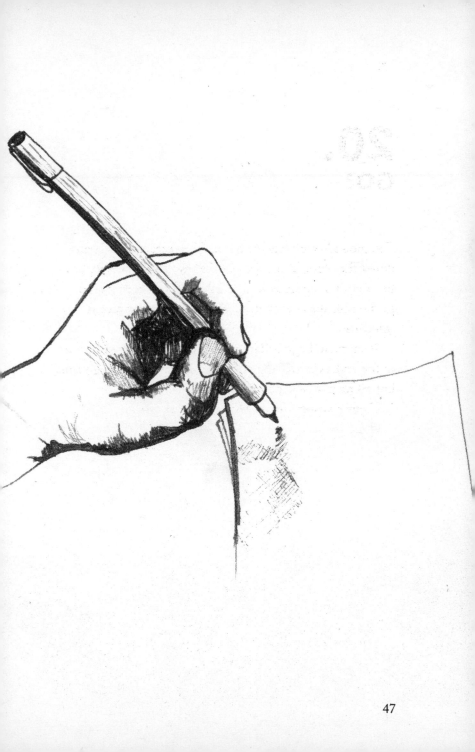

BUILDING
CHARACTER

21.
START WITH CHARACTERS OR START WITH PLOT?

In simple terms, there are two kinds of writing: the character-driven variety and the plot-driven variety. Character-driven writing is usually associated with literary fiction, and plot-driven writing with genre fiction (see section 3).

A good example of character-driven writing would be something like a Chekhov short story. A girl in a dacha wonders whether or not to get married. Nothing happens to her and then it ends ('Life's a birch and then you die').

An example of plot-driven writing would be something like *Goldfinger* by Ian Fleming. A madman wishes to control the world's gold reserves and likes covering women with gold paint. Conflict, action, climax, post-coital cigarette.

However, even in a Chekhov story there is usually a plot of some sort. The characters may undergo some sort of internal, psychic change, which may have important consequences for what happens. Chekhov's story 'The Black Monk' follows the descent into madness of a young

Russian professor, and charts the destruction he wreaks among those who love him. And in thrillers there are usually strong characters. In *Goldfinger* the characters are extremely memorable, even if they are caricatures.

So the distinction is largely a false one. Stephen King, a genre writer, said: 'Plot is the good writer's last resort and the dullard's first choice.' An over-reliance on plot can produce something stilted which ultimately fails to grip even the most action-hungry reader.

The truth is that characters and plot are aspects of one another – like matter and energy. Henry James said: 'What is character but the determination of incident? What is incident but the illumination of character?' In other words, the kind of people your characters are determines what they do (which becomes the plot); and how they react to the events of the plot reveals the kind of people they are (thus showing their character). It's a circle. The plot is impossible without the characters and the characters without the plot.

Feel free to consider your characters first or your plot first – just don't forget to consider both. Your readers will be expecting you to.

22.
DRAFT A 'CHARACTER CV'

Before you start writing, it's useful to know as much as possible about each of your main characters. You can tabulate this information in the form of a 'character CV' for each one.

You probably won't use all the information you gather – in fact, you probably won't use most of it – but it will help you nevertheless. For example, once you've made it your business to find out everything you can, you'll find that your characters will only act in certain ways. They will resist being asked to act 'out of character'. This is the fabled moment when the characters take over – but it's a product of hard work and not of magic.

You'll also find that new paths open up. For example, let's say you give your character a more successful older sibling. What does this now mean, psychologically, for your character? He/she might now feel something of a family black sheep. This might influence their behaviour, and then conceivably influence the plot.

Consider the following areas:

- Your character's name (see section 35);
- Their appearance (eye colour, shape of nose, mouth, teeth, ears, hair and hairstyle, facial hair, body shape, height, any remarkable physical characteristics, gestures, own private feelings about their body, manner of speech);
- Their dress (general style of dress, lower body dress, upper body dress, shoes, jewellery, other);
- Their personal and social statistics (date of birth, age, nationality, place of birth, social class);
- Their family (their parents, living or dead, their parents' marital status, parents' occupation, step-parents if any, siblings if any, children if any, names and ages of children);
- Their education and work history (school, further education, job history, current job);
- Their relationships (sexuality, relationship history, relationship status, marital status, partner's name and other details, social life/friends);
- Their other personality characteristics (religion, politics, hobbies and interests, taste in art, taste in literature, taste in music, private fears, weaknesses, strengths, particular dislikes/phobias, particular likes/passions, health problems, general demeanour).

This will seem like hard work while you're doing it. It may also feel slightly tangential, as if you're not actually getting on with the real business of writing. But it is likely to be one of the best investments you will ever make in producing a novel.

23.
REDUCE YOUR CHARACTERS TO TIERS

It would be time-consuming and counter-productive to make up a CV for every character. Some characters are frankly unimportant. They exist only to move the plot on or act as a foil to the main character.

It's useful to think of characters in tiers, like a wedding cake. At the top tier is your main character or characters. There's usually only room for one or two (see the next section). The reader spends a lot of time with the main characters and cares what happens to them. Events are often seen from their point of view. They develop and change. They are 'round' rather than 'flat' (see section 25).

On the next level are the fully-fleshed out supporting cast. They also appear frequently in the story and have a close connection with the main character(s). We know a lot about them and empathize with them, and may see things from their point of view. But the novel is not quite their story.

On the third level are the minor characters. These are drawn in a few strokes and we don't feel particularly close to them. They could appear a few times but their story is not important: they can be left hanging there, their dilemmas and problems unresolved, when the novel finishes. We probably won't see things from their point of view.

On the fourth level are characters mentioned only in passing: street musicians, bar-staff, librarians, those who may contribute something tangential to the plot but are never mentioned again. (There is nothing intrinsically minor about a librarian, naturally – but unless they scan your barcode with a particularly significant flourish they are likely to remain firmly in the background.)

24.
UNDERSTAND THE JOB OF THE MAIN CHARACTER

In a novel, it's fair to say that the main character is everything. If the main character is boring or unconvincing, the novel will fail. If he is vivid and unique, the novel may succeed.

The main character will also tend to determine the degree of emotional investment the reader has in the novel. Readers want novels to move them (see section 84). This means that the main character should be sympathetic to some extent. He can have plenty of flaws – like Pechorin in Lermontov's ironically-titled *A Hero of Our Time*, for example – but unless he is also in some way likable or admirable we are unlikely to make that emotional investment.

There will probably be only one main character in an average-sized novel – or two at the most. Any more and the sense of focus will dissipate. It's hard to move a plot forward when each of several characters must be given equal weight as a co-hero or co-heroine. There can be subsidiary characters too, of course – fully-fleshed-out ones, with many 'main-character' attributes – but the story is not theirs.

What are the attributes of a main character? PG Wodehouse said that their primary attribute was that they act. He wrote:

> What a vital thing it is to have plenty of things for a major character to do. If they aren't in interesting situations, characters can't be major characters, not even if you have the rest of the troupe talk their heads off about them.

Wodehouse often thought of his characters as actors (he wrote dozens of musicals) and he had noticed that important actors would often walk out of a production if they thought their character wasn't given good enough lines. So he treated his fictional characters the same, as if they were prima donna actors: he pampered them, gave them good lines and made sure they were in the thick of the action.

Acting by itself isn't quite good enough however. It should be significant action. It should drive the plot forward. The main character should make choices that determine the way things develop. In this sense, main characters are in control, even if they don't realize it themselves.

A final attribute of the main character is to do with point of view (see section 69 onwards). The novel is their story, and the point of view will reflect that fact. We may even inhabit the main character's head for the whole novel.

25.
DEPLOY MINOR CHARACTERS

On the second tier of the cake we find the supporting cast, who have many of the same attributes of the main character(s) but do not primarily drive the action. And then on the third tier of the cake, we find the minor characters.

EM Forster in his *Aspects of the Novel* called these minor characters 'flat' characters, as distinct from 'round' ones. 'Flat' characters are ones with just one or two traits. Think of the characters that swarm in Dickens. Would it have added to our pleasure if every single one of them had been made into a convincing human being? Probably not. We are much more entertained by them, in fact, as the embodiment of a couple of traits. They can then be trundled onstage to perform their piece, then trundled off, leaving the stage to the 'round' characters, who are richly developed and perhaps a little unpredictable (compare Norman Mailer's definition of 'beings' in section 28). As Forster put it:

The test of a round character is whether it is capable of surprising in a convincing way. If it never surprises, it is flat. If it does not convince, it is flat pretending to be round.

Flat, cardboard characters can be useful, therefore. Deploy cardboard for the effects it can bring you, and then have your hero come crashing through the cardboard scenery when he takes centre stage.

26.
OBSERVE YOURSELF

So far I've talked about getting to know your characters, ordering them in tiers of significance, and deploying them in your work.

But what if you struggle to think up characters? What if you have no imagination?

Firstly, everyone has an imagination. Some of us might have trouble accessing it on certain days, but everyone daydreams and fantasizes, often in a quite riotous and unabashed fashion.

However, if you are not in a daydreaming mood, and you need something right now, in front of your computer or notebook – what do you do?

Let's say that one of your characters is a possessive, jealous wife. You don't know how to get under her skin. She won't 'come alive'. One solution to the problem is simply to look at yourself. Ask yourself: When was the last time you got jealous? How did you feel? Ratchet the feeling up a couple of notches. Never mind that you're not married (or not a woman). Build on what you experienced: take those small stirrings of suspicion and imagine how you would feel if they were the dominant forces in your life. You'd go through his things, wouldn't you? You'd follow him? You'd check his email? The speedometer on his car?

In a way you have to become a good actor, impersonating your characters. No actor on the stage has the benefit of having been every conceivable character: they must bootstrap themselves into the role of a lover, or an industrialist, or a cowgirl. One useful thing to do is to imagine you are such an actor, and speak aloud the lines you have written for your character, perhaps in their accent, so that you 'sound' like them. Ridiculous as it may seem, it actually works: if you speak one line, it will magically suggest another. You start to become that person.

Of course, as a writer you have the luxury of being able to start from anywhere; so if you really can't become a possessive wife, you can write her out.

In any case, observation of yourself and your own experiences is only a starting-point. You must adapt real life. You must bring in all sorts of other factors: motivation, conflict, point of view, setting, period. If your possessive wife has her own lover she may experience a conflict of interest; or if she lives in eighteenth-century England she may have no legal recourse and will therefore have to take the law into her own hands. Take the kernel of your own experiences and transform them.

27.
OBSERVE OTHER PEOPLE

When William Burroughs was asked to give advice to
a young writer, he replied: 'For Godsake, keep your eyes
open. Notice what's going on around you.'

It's certainly easier to write novels if you are interested
in your surroundings, and this means being interested
in other people and their lives. If other people frighten,
disgust or bore you, you will have a harder time inventing
characters (which are the basis of novels). Observing
people, talking to them and getting to know them will give
you many of your best ideas.

However, it's wise to resist the immediate temptation
to put your friends, family or colleagues into your stories.
They will not thank you for it. They will regard it as an
invasion of privacy and may feel 'used', especially if you
have included private or confidential information. Even if
you take care to change details and cover your tracks, they
will see through your efforts and may even see references
to themselves if there is no intention to depict them.
AL Kennedy said: 'It might be better to celebrate those
you love – and love itself – by writing in such a way that

everyone keeps their privacy and dignity intact.'

Casual acquaintances and strangers are different, because less is at stake. But here again you should be careful: if you do use a real person as a starting-point, bear in mind that a starting-point is just that – it's a point from which you start. In one of my novels I based a character on a man I met on a plane. He was a larger-than-life figure with a loud, annoying voice and was strikingly dishevelled in appearance. As I worked up the character, I decided to give him a special gift to act as a counterweight to his failings: I made him an expert draughtsman. This became crucial to the book. Then I added some characteristics of another person I knew slightly. I changed his background (or what I knew of his background). I began to investigate, in my own imagination, his family, his tastes, his job history. Before long I had created someone entirely new, someone I knew much better than I had ever known the man on the plane.

For this is what you must do to any 'found' character: change them. Real life is always inadequate for the purposes of storytelling: you need to adapt it (see section 29). Observe people carefully, but carefully select from what you have observed. Knowing a person's motivation for what they have said or done can be crucial (see section 33). It's only when, as a novelist, you get inside a character and understand his hidden depths and desires that you can take a 'found' detail and make it into a satisfying piece of fiction.

28.

USE THE NORMAN MAILER METHOD

Norman Mailer used a technique similar to the one I have just described. In an interview he explained the process whereby he turned a real person into a fictional one:

> I try to put the model in situations which have very little to do with his real situations in life. Very quickly the model disappears. His private reality can't hold up. For instance, I might take somebody who is a professional football player, a man let's say whom I know slightly, and make him a movie star. In a transposition of this sort, everything which relates particularly to the professional football player quickly disappears, and what is left, curiously, is what is exportable in his character. But this process while interesting in the early stages is not as exciting as the more creative act of allowing your characters to grow once they're separated from the model. It's once they become almost as

complex as one's own personality that the fine excitement begins. Because then they are not really characters any longer – they're beings.

Mailer describes the process of transposition and transformation, but also draws a distinction between 'characters' and 'beings'. Characters are those people who you have a clear handle on; beings, however, are more disturbingly like real people in that they can change, be contradictory, be unpredictable, be, in fact, 'almost as complex as one's own personality'. And once you've created a character who is almost as complex as Norman Mailer, you know you've struck gold.

29.
ADAPT REAL LIFE

There are essential differences between what happens in life and what happens in books. You only have to look at what novels are for. They are there to entertain us, whereas real life is not often very entertaining. They create meaning, whereas real life often seems meaningless. They provide escape, but what are we trying to escape from? Real life, naturally.

Even dramatic happenings from real life, such as car crashes and mafia hits, may still be weak in novelistic terms unless they are integrated into a gripping story.

Here are some ways to adapt real life:

• Change the point of view. Make your real-life event happen to any of various characters in your novel and see how they respond. Remember, you should always have an eye on how the real-life event illuminates characters or contributes to the plot.
• Use any 'found' dialogue, but bear in mind that real dialogue is often circuitous, pointless, repetitive, and full of false starts and hesitations. Adapt it so that it

illuminates character or moves the plot forward. If there's no dialogue in your real story, include some. For more advice on dialogue, see section 61.

• Make sure you look for the emotional angle (see section 84). The novels you have enjoyed the most almost certainly moved you in some way to wonder, terror, amusement, pity, excitement. Aim to reproduce the same effects.

• Make your real-life story suspenseful by asking interesting questions and withholding details (see section 38).

• Include conflicts between characters as a cause or result of the real-life event. If the event is a car crash, for example, make the driver of the car the adulterous lover of the passenger. Invest events with significance.

In most cases, a novelist's job is not to transcribe a 'slice of life' onto the page, unworked and unchanged. There is almost always the potential for improvement. Why else would people 'embellish' stories when they tell them? Don't force yourself to keep to 'what really happened' out of loyalty to real life. A novel is not a biography or a newspaper article. It is a different beast, and satisfies different desires.

30.
USE PHOTOS

Later on I suggest that you use pictures or other graphic elements as part of your book. What I am suggesting here, by contrast, is that you use pictures or photos as a starting-point to build character.

Pictures, and especially photos of people, can be very powerful in suggesting character traits. As human beings we instinctually read a great deal into people's appearances. Faces, hairstyles, manners of dress, posture and gesture imply a great deal; we make many unconscious assumptions as soon as we meet someone (many of which might later turn out to be wrong, of course), and the same applies to the way we interpret a photo. It's possible to build an entire character from one photo.

One way to go about it is to have a certain character in mind to start with. If, for example, you've decided that he works as a mechanic, have a look for photos of mechanics. The internet has made this kind of search much easier – but it's also possible you may find what you want in newspapers or magazines. When you have found a likely-looking photo, print or clip it out and put it with your 'character CV'. Refer to it as you interrogate your character. Ask him: What are your secret fears? Who are your parents? How many GCSEs do you have? What sort of music do you like? You will see the answers in his eyes.

It's possible to start even further back than this. A single image from a magazine can suggest all sorts of possibilities, some of which could be crucial to your plot. A girl in an old-fashioned coat stands on a pier holding a Brownie camera. Why is she there? When was the photo taken? Who is she photographing? Why don't the other people seem to notice her? Get into the habit of asking yourself these kinds of questions about what lies behind a photo.

Try building up a scrap file of photos for inspirational purposes. Landscapes, townscapes, streetscapes, interiors, people, crowds, animals, vehicles, meetings, celebrations. If you see something you like, print or clip it out for later reference.

A picture is only worth a thousand words if someone takes the trouble to interpret it.

31.
INTRODUCE YOUR CHARACTERS

You will have noticed that the first time a character appears in a novel, there is a description of their appearance. This first description introduces the character and fixes him or her in our minds.

There are several ways of giving an introductory description of a character. A long exposition à la George Eliot, giving every detail of a person's face, figure, dress, etc., is fine, but may feel a little dated. There are other methods.

A description of a person engaged in some characteristic action – such as playing basketball or addressing a meeting – is often effective. This way, the character is introduced doing something *characteristic*. We observe the character's grace, her confidence – or lack of it. We get a sense of not just how she looks but how she lives.

Or a character may look in a mirror and describe him or herself. This moves the description away from exposition and into the character's own self-image: it is part action and part 'reflection'.

A character may have a vision of him or herself.

On the first page of *Pictures of Fidelman* by Bernard Malamud, the main character, Arthur Fidelman, feeling very self-conscious on arriving in a new city, has a sudden intense sense of himself as others see him. Again, this gives psychological layering to a straight description. A character may also enter a room full of people who all turn to look, giving the character a sense of how others judge him, which he then communicates to the reader.

A character may be described in the thoughts or comments of others. 'You look exhausted' is more interesting than saying 'She was exhausted'.

A character may be described by association with some other object. A middle-aged man who arrives on a large motorcycle or a young man who walks down the road reading *Ariel* by Sylvia Plath give us a strong sense of who these characters are as human beings.

And there are other methods. What you must bear in mind is that simple authorial description is not the only way to approach the task.

One note of caution: if, after having introduced the character, you then leave several pages before giving some new and vital piece of information about their appearance, the reader will feel puzzled. 'Flame-red hair? A missing nose? Why wasn't this mentioned earlier?'

32.
GIVE YOUR CHARACTERS HIDDEN DEPTHS

Imagine the following scenario: a teacher is well known for dealing sternly with her students. But when she gets home she gets drunk and weeps. She talks to her neighbour and confesses her fears of old age and redundancy.

The story can also go in reverse: imagine a teacher who is much loved by her students. But when she gets home she beats her children if they don't study...

These examples show that the way someone appears on the surface can be very different from the way they are underneath. This is as true in art as it is in life. The task of the novel can be to reveal this difference and make it understandable – understandable in both senses, that of 'comprehensible' and 'forgivable'.

However, once the difference has been revealed, what do you do? Leave the character with this dichotomy, this split personality? If you do, there will be no drama. The character will be split, yes, but static. The challenge now is to force them to confront their hidden reality, their inner demons.

This can provide you with a potent plot for a novel (see section 39 below on using character to generate plot). The teacher who fears old age and redundancy can be made to face her terrors, and in the process change as a person. The teacher who is much loved by her students can also be forced into a crisis: perhaps she will be observed, in public, hitting her children, and be seen for what she is. She will come to a realization of her poor parenting and be forced to mend her ways.

It is when characters are forced into intolerable positions that the difference between how they appear and how they really are comes out. This is the crucible you must provide for them.

In one of my novels I orchestrated a crisis in a character's life simply by making them lose their medication. There are many other ways to do it: characters can be forced to respond to someone choking in a restaurant, deal with an unexpected responsibility for someone's pet, lose the one thing they love.

Your job as a novelist, in fact, is that of chief torturer. Traumatize your characters and the hidden depths will come screaming to the surface. Then make your characters deal with the result. This is the stuff of drama.

33.
MAKE YOUR CHARACTERS WANT SOMETHING

In the previous section I talked about giving your character hidden depths: that is, revealing what they are really like, underneath what they merely seem to be like.

However, there is a deeper issue even than this. Why are they like this? Why does the teacher beat her children? Is it because she was beaten as a child? Is it because she will feel a failure if her children are not successful?

These sorts of questions are to do with motivation.

Kurt Vonnegut said: 'Every character should want something, even if it is only a glass of water.' In one of Vonnegut's novels, *Breakfast of Champions*, a minor character, a waitress, desires more than anything else in the world to have white-walled tyres for her car. This leads her to behave in certain ways – to be nice even to people who are unpleasant to her, hoping for tips to buy her tyres with – which, as it turns out, has consequences for what happens in the story. Motivation, therefore, can drive plot.

When we know what characters want, their actions take on a completely new meaning. If we know that someone steals a bicycle to get a job to save his family from penury (as in the film *The Bicycle Thieves*), we are more sympathetic to them than if we think they are a casual thief who will later dump the bike in a canal.

If you know what your characters want you can also put obstacles in their path, and so create drama. As I said in the previous section, your role as an author is that of chief torturer. Make your character's dream seem possible, then snatch it away from them. Tantalize them. Let's say your character wants to be respected: well, then, your job is to humiliate them (the plot of *Disgrace* by JM Coetzee). Find out what they hate and fear, what they are powerfully motivated to reject and run away from, and inflict it on them. See how they react. If your hero has a phobia of lifts, stick him in one. (Your readers will be expecting you to stick him in one, and will be let down if you don't.) More subtly, if he fears loneliness he can be stuck alone in a lift. If he fears pain he can be exposed to the pain of others.

Motivation can be considered in the same way as the 'character CV' I referred to above (see section 22). That is, it's important that you know what a character's motives are, even if the reader doesn't. You don't always need to reveal motivation, since it may not always be the main driver of the plot. However, knowing your character's motivations lends richness to your understanding of them.

34.
SHOW CHANGE IN YOUR CHARACTERS

This is perhaps the most artificial thing you will ever do to your characters – show them changing. People in real life often don't change very much, especially after they've passed the age of twenty-five. We all know people who seem positively incapable of change, as if they've been programmed to behave in certain ways, and can't, or don't want to, escape from their destiny.

Characters in novels, on the other hand, almost always change in some way. They go on a 'journey'; they realize their true role in life; they change their partners, professions, allegiances, nationalities, sexualities. They are redeemed or destroyed. Why do we believe it?

The first reason is that we, as readers, want to believe that people can change, even if the evidence shows that they often can't. We have a hunger for change in our own lives. We want things to improve, want wrongs to be righted; we also wish, in our own lives, for the excitement of change, for the humdrum world we inhabit to fall away. It is a powerful element of the 'escapist' nature of novels that they show, plausibly, that change can and does happen in the lives of ordinary people.

The second reason we swallow so much change in novels is that change is an essential part of everything novels are. In a sense, without change, there would be no novel.

Novelists know that in order to create satisfying stories there must be conflict (see section 40). As a result they deliberately put challenges and obstacles into their characters' lives – deaths, accidents, discoveries, betrayals. In coping with these challenges and obstacles the character is forced to make choices, often under extreme pressure. As they do so, their inner resources are tested, and their hidden depths come out (as we have just seen). All of this – challenges and obstacles, conflicts, choices, the emergence of hidden depths, leads inexorably to one thing: change. If the character simply remained the same after all that, it wouldn't be believable. Characters have to change, because novelists insist on poking, goading and tormenting them.

In summary, then, when characters in a novel change, they change for two reasons: because readers want to read about change, and because they have been provoked into change by the exigencies of the novel form itself.

35.
NAME YOUR CHARACTERS

'A good name,' said the English clergyman William Jenkyn, 'is a thread tied about the finger, to make us mindful of the errand we came into the world to do for our Master.' Names weave a sort of magic, whether Christian, pagan or otherwise. They are strangely bound up with the identities of things. It has been said that for each of us the most magical word in the language is our own name.

The names you choose for your characters will be very important, and it is worth giving them careful thought. You should consider a number of things. Firstly, names should be appropriate to the time and place you are writing about. Very few girls were named Agatha or Enid in the 1960s, and even fewer named Summer or Gaia in the 1920s. Try consulting tables of the most popular names from the period you are writing about. Similarly with names from particular places: take some time to research the most popular names in the relevant places or countries. Best of all, consult a native speaker on this matter; they will often be able to say if a name sounds 'wrong'.

Secondly, your names should be appropriate.

Appropriateness takes two forms: appropriateness to the character and appropriateness to the style of the book. The name Algernon might suggest stiff old-fashioned attitudes (though naming a drunken tramp Algernon will benefit greatly from a sense of incongruity). A woman called Rockette will probably have a history.

Appropriateness to the style of the book is another issue. If you are writing a comedy you can have more fun with names. But even in a realistic novel there is room for suggestive experimentation: e.g. the polyamorous 'Rabbit' Angstrom in John Updike's *Rabbit, Run* or the uniquely-named Heathcliff in Emily Brontë's *Wuthering Heights*.

Thirdly, the various names you choose should be fairly easy to distinguish from each other. If you are writing about a group of three friends, don't call them Ben, Bob and Bill (and the two greatest adversaries in world politics should not be called Obama and Osama).

I would recommend you be as imaginative as you dare with names. Real life always outdoes anything you will find in fiction anyway. Leslie Thomas wrote a book called *The Adventures of Goodnight and Loving*, about a bored solicitor, George Goodnight, who leaves his job and heads out on a series of round-the-world travels, encountering various ladies on the way (with whom the 'loving' occurs). The title is named after two real nineteenth-century cowboys, Charles Goodnight and Oliver Loving, who pioneered a real cattle trail in New Mexico, the Goodnight-Loving Trail. In this case, the plot of the book, its title, and the appeal of its central idea rests crucially on these two unlikely names.

36.
NAME EVERYTHING ELSE

When you write, you'll find yourself not only having to name people, but many other things. Writing a novel is like being one of the first colonists of the New World. These pioneers had to find names for mountains, rivers, trees, animals, etc., and while some were conservative (Jamaica is divided into three counties called Middlesex, Surrey and Cornwall), others were downright anarchic (there are Mid-Western towns called Knockemstiff, Lizard Lick, Monkey's Eyebrow, and Embarrass). As a novelist you should be capable of invention across the spectrum, producing conservative names when conservatism is called for and outrageous names when you think you can get away with it.

It's perhaps unlikely that you'll feel it necessary to name a species of animal in your novel. But you may well have to name an individual animal. What about an annoying Chihuahua? Candy? Munchkin? The Tiny Defaecator? What would you call a fanzine? Or a set of quadruplets? Or a new political party? Or a provincial newspaper? Or a chocolate bar? Or a nail bar? Or a tapas bar? Or a lost play by Shakespeare? Or a lost language of the ancient Matto Grosso?

As with the names of characters, careful thought about the names of things will reap dividends. The right name will leap off the page and give your readers a feeling of pleasurable recognition; they will consequently feel more confident in surrendering themselves to your fictional world.

BUILDING PLOT

37.
HOW DO YOU INVENT A PLOT?

Inventing a plot is easy. It's possible to generate a simple plot with just three ingredients:

- a character;
- a desire;
- an obstacle.

You can even do it as a parlour game. Write down four characters on four pieces of paper. They might be: a computer programmer, a ballerina, a struggling artist, a tea-taster. Then four desires in a new pile: to write a novel, to get away for the weekend, to find true love, to visit the Himalayas. Then four obstacles in another pile: the neighbours are noisy, the garage roof has collapsed, the library is shut, there's no food in the house. Now shuffle each pile and take one piece of paper from each:

A struggling artist wants to visit the Himalayas but the neighbours are noisy.

Now comes the important part. Your job is to find a way

of connecting the character, the desire and the obstacle, and then finding a resolution that involves change in the character. (Showing your characters changing is very important to plots, as we have seen.)

So, for example: the struggling artist wants to visit the Himalayas, to paint them. He's saving up for the trip and has to get up early to do his dead-end job, but his neighbours are noisy and making it impossible to sleep. One evening he decides to confront them. To his surprise, they invite him in and he joins the party. He tells them about his dream of painting the Himalayas, but he realizes, as he speaks the words, that the dream is unrealistic: he hasn't thought it through at all, and hates the cold and camping. What he really wants, he realizes, is someone to talk to. Once he puts his Himalayan dream in words it evaporates. He's changed.

This is the plot of a short story rather than a novel, but it's possible to build a novel from a repetition of these structures. What if the artist, now aware that he really needs friends more than anything else, decides to make fifty new friends that year? How would he fare? There will be plenty more obstacles to deal with, and plenty more changes and realizations as he undertakes his new journey in search of friendship.

In fact, boil it all down, and the hero is on a quest. Some have seen this as the basic plot of all novels. The hero might be seeking friendship, love, money, truth, justice, fame, but ultimately it is all a quest. On the way, he has to overcome many challenges, and when he arrives at his goal, he is a different person from when he started.

38.
UNDERSTAND SUSPENSE AND MYSTERY

You might well think that the foregoing is a bit simplistic. Can all plots really be boiled down to a quest? Surprisingly, they often can. Charles Dickens' *Great Expectations* is a quest for social improvement; Anita Loos' *Gentlemen Prefer Blondes* is a quest for diamonds; David Hughes' *The Pork Butcher* is a quest to atone for war guilt; Hanif Kureishi's *Intimacy* is a quest for personal and sexual freedom.

But there are other ingredients to plots too – and among the most crucial are suspense and mystery.

A couple of definitions:

• A suspense plot is one in which the reader wonders: what will happen? (Example: a bomb will explode unless money is paid within 24 hours.)
• A mystery plot is one in which the reader wonders: how did this happen? (Example: a body has been discovered in the library and no one knows who the murderer is.)

Suspense deals with events that will happen and mystery deals with events that have happened. Both types of plots, you will notice, involve the withholding of information. In a suspense plot we keep reading because we want to know how obstacles can be overcome or how the hero can get out of jeopardy; in a mystery plot we keep reading because we want a solution to a puzzle. The withholding of crucial information in both cases generates tension in the reader, and the release of tension is pleasurable when the information finally arrives.

Here's an interesting question, though: if readers simply want information, why don't they just turn to the end of the book?

Well, sometimes they do, because the intervening pages don't grab them enough. If, however, the author has created engaging characters to populate his pages – characters we care about and sympathize with – then the reader is persuaded to stay with the book and not take the easy way out.

Again, it all comes back to character. There may be a body in the library, and there may be a murderer on the loose, but without good characters, finding out why and who is no more emotionally engaging than doing a sudoku puzzle. Character is what makes the journey of the book emotionally satisfying and meaningful.

39.
USE CHARACTER TO GENERATE PLOT

A couple of pages ago I suggested that you can create a simple plot from three ingredients that can be gathered almost randomly: a character, a desire and some obstacles. Link them together and provide a resolution that involves change in the character, and hey presto, you have a plot.

However, you probably won't go about creating a plot in this 'parlour game' way. You may already have a developed character in mind, and won't want a tea-taster or an airline steward foisted on you.

If you do have a character already in mind, then, and know them quite well – you may already have written a 'character CV' for them, as in section 22 – you can use this character to begin generating your plot.

For example, what does your character look like? If they are strikingly beautiful or ugly, how will that influence the way people behave towards them? What are their fears? Fears are great plot-generators. The things that characters fear can be inflicted on them, to see which way they twitch. What are their ambitions and motivations?

These are also great plot-generators (remember Vonnegut: 'Every character should want something, even if it is only a glass of water'). What is their social class? Their personal wealth? Take the following scenario: a builder, of humble origins, makes good and buys a Rolls Royce. Once day he's out driving it when some youths in a lorry start to jeer. He rams the lorry with the Rolls. He gets out and... it could end in a number of ways, but it would all come from knowing about the man's origins.

Character is plot, and plot character: that is all ye know on earth, and all ye need to know.

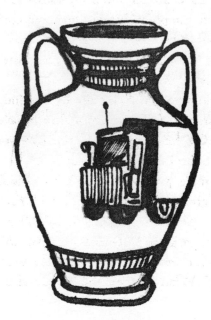

40.
CREATE CONFLICT

If you think of a novel as a big clockwork machine, with lots of wheels and gears, then the wheel labelled 'conflict' is the biggest wheel, right at the heart of the mechanism.

Call to mind any successful novel and there will be conflict in abundance. *Moby-Dick* presents the conflict between Ahab and the White Whale; *Chocolat* by Joanne Harris presents the conflict between Vianne Rocher and Francis Reynaud; *Alice's Adventures in Wonderland* presents the conflict between Alice and the phantasms of her dream-world. Imagine these novels with no conflict – if Ahab caught and killed the White Whale on page five, if Vianne and M. Reynaud got along famously, or if everyone and everything Alice met was nice and perfectly reasonable. Without conflict it's impossible to generate suspense, to bring about change in characters, to reveal their hidden depths, or to get readers emotionally involved.

Conflict can be thought of as occurring on three possible levels: inner, inter- and outer.

Inner conflict happens as a result of dilemmas within a character's heart or mind. A character may wonder, for example, whether to stay with her marriage for the sake of the kids; or whether to help a friend, despite the fact that it may bring disaster on her own head. If this sort of dilemma is presented convincingly enough, readers will be as much on the edge of their seats as they would watching an action movie.

The second level ('inter-' or interpersonal) is between characters. This might take the form of violent, implacable opposition, as in a crime or war novel, or something subtler: misunderstandings or attempts by characters to pull in different directions. Conflict between characters is also widely used for comic effect.

The third type of conflict is outer, as a result of environmental or societal forces ranged against the character (fire, flood, disaster, disapproval, poverty, oppression). This is often seen in the novel of adventure, or in the so-called *bildungsroman* – the novel of an individual's development from youth to maturity.

Often there will be conflict on more than one level. A detective may want to catch a serial killer but is at the same time haunted by his inner demons (inner and inter-). A nuclear engineer may wish to prevent an environmental disaster but is opposed by his superiors who wish to implement safety cutbacks (outer and inter-). A young man may wish to discover himself spiritually but struggles to cope in the big city (inner and outer).

41.
ANTICIPATE THE CLIMAX

The princess will fall into a hundred-year sleep if she pricks her finger on the spindle of a spinning-wheel. So the king bans all spinning wheels from the kingdom. We know what's coming: the princess, silly girl, will still, somehow, manage to find a spinning wheel. It's only a matter of time.

It's important to let readers know what's coming. A surprise that is not prepared for, rather paradoxically, has rather less impact than a surprise we know is going to occur. Imagine a horror story in which there was no building of atmosphere, no dread of what might lurk round the corner. When the hideous climax arrived, wouldn't the impact be reduced?

In novels, the reader is often alerted to the arrival of a climactic scene by the inclusion of smaller prefigurations of the same event. For example, if the climactic scene is a mugging, there can be a report of a mugging earlier on, and the characters can then be given the opportunity to react to it, to discuss their fears, to prepare themselves and the reader for such an eventuality.

In *The Outsider* by Albert Camus, there are numerous occasions in which the narrator, Meursault, is shown exhibiting a detached, emotionally uninvolved attitude to life. For example, at the beginning of the book, his mother dies and he tells the porter at the funeral home that he doesn't wish to view the body:

> 'Eh? What's that? [the porter] exclaimed. 'You don't want me to...'
> 'No,' I said.
> He put the screwdriver back in his pocket and stared at me.

Later Meursault writes a letter to a young woman on behalf of a friend, knowing that if the girl responds to the letter, the friend will beat her up:

> I wrote the letter. I didn't take much trouble over it, but I wanted to satisfy Raymond, as I had no reason not to satisfy him.

When Meursault finally kills a man, pumping five shots into his body, he can give no adequate reason for what he has done. But by now we've had numerous opportunities to see that Meursault is a peculiarly unempathetic person, and that the action, in its own terms, makes perfect sense.

Let your novel's minor events prefigure the major ones, and your readers will be able to savour those major events to the full.

42.
RESOLVE CONFLICT

In section 37 I put together a simple plot, randomly generated from three elements. In its final form it involved an artist who realizes he's lonely and sets himself the task of making fifty friends before the year is out.

Let's take this story forward a little. The artist faces numerous problems in his quest for friends, chief among them the forces in his own nature that have made him friendless in the first place. But finally, there is a climax in which all the conflicts – inner, inter- and perhaps outer – explode at the moment of the deadline.

The plot could develop in any number of ways. On December 31st (or whenever the deadline is), the artist, despairing of finding fifty friends, might 'hire' a large number of people to pretend to be his friends, only to make a speech on the night of the deadline, revealing that he has cheated. This would represent a substantial change in his character, perhaps impelled by his desire to be true to the one real friend he has found. Alternatively he might be forced into a confrontation with an antagonist who wishes to frustrate him in his quest. In the showdown, the artist draws on his inner resources and his real self comes out.

As the climax of any story arrives, the forces set into motion by the conflicts of the plot collide. The protagonist either triumphs or is overwhelmed. The resolution is a result of this climax. Now there is no more narrative tension; it is dissipated and disappears. By the end of the story all the loose ends – at least as far as they relate to the major character(s) – have been tied up. There is a sense of conclusion. The test is ultimately this: is the reader left at the end thinking: 'Yes, and what happens next?' Hopefully not. Resolution means the story is over. A new story might be beginning, but the story of the novel is wrapped up.

What's more, in the best case, the resolution has emerged from character. The most satisfying resolutions are not foisted on characters, but come from the journey of the novel and the people the characters have become. If the conflicts have been resolved in a forced, 'bolted-on' manner, the reader won't believe it. If the character has previously been shown as inflexible and unreflective, for example, a sudden change of heart at the end of the novel, for no apparent reason, is likely to be treated with contempt and the novel flung across the room.

43.

TWIST THE PLOT

As you build your plot, you may find that you are not content merely with bringing everything to an orderly and logical conclusion. You may wish to surprise your readers. Plot twists are often found in detective fiction or other sorts of mystery or suspense fiction, but they are also found in so-called literary fiction (see section 3).

One type of twist has already been mentioned: the revelation that the narrator is unreliable (see section 71). In this sort of twist, we discover that the narrator has falsified key aspects of the information presented to the reader. The discovery that the narrator is unreliable may come at the end of the novel (*Atonement* by Ian McEwan is a celebrated example), or may become more and more obvious as the book progresses.

A sudden and unexpected change in the character's circumstances can also supply a twist ending. This can be positive or negative. If positive it could lead to an unexpectedly happy ending; if negative it could take the form of a 'hoist by his own petard' or 'caught in his own trap' type of plot.

A sudden recognition of the reality of things, or the true nature of people, can also supply a twist ending. In Macbeth, for example, the hero believes himself to be invulnerable, until Macduff reveals that he was 'from the womb untimely ripped'.

A 'red herring' plot might also supply a twist. Red herrings are particularly associated with detective fiction. (The term 'red herring' itself probably comes from an article of 1807 by William Cobbett in which he says how, as a boy, he had used a kipper, or red herring, to throw hounds off the scent of a hare.) For example, we might strongly suspect one character of having committed a murder, because of certain clues inserted into the text, but the only reason the clues are there is to deflect attention from the real murderer, a mousy character whose true evil comes out in a surprise climax.

All of these techniques can be useful, but one rule of thumb worth bearing in mind is: don't use 'deus ex machina' twists (see section 45). The sudden reversal will be most effective if it emerges out of character. Mousy characters must have real motives for murder; unreliable narrators must have real reasons for manipulating events; people caught in their own traps should be caught because of their own arrogance or complacency.

44.
TRY A MACGUFFIN

The term 'MacGuffin' was popularized, if not invented, by
Alfred Hitchcock. A MacGuffin refers to an element of
the plot – often an object – which dominates the lives and
motivations of the characters, and which drives the story
forward. Hitchcock explained it like this:

> We have a name in the studio, and we call it the
> 'MacGuffin'. It is the mechanical element that
> usually crops up in any story. In crook stories it is
> almost always the necklace and in spy stories it is
> most always the papers.

One characteristic of the MacGuffin is that it may not have
much bearing on the central events of the plot. An example
in cinema would be 'Rosebud' in *Citizen Kane*. The film
opens with the dying Kane whispering the word 'Rosebud',
and continues as people try to find out what Kane could
have meant. Finally it's revealed (spoiler here) that 'Rosebud'
was the name of Kane's boyhood sledge – which has
nothing in particular to do with the plot.

This device can be exploited in novels too. The doubloon that Ahab nails to the mast in *Moby-Dick* is a sort of MacGuffin, since it motivates the crew, yet no one finally claims it; Magnus Mills' novels are full of MacGuffins, objects that intrude with dreamlike significance into the lives of the characters – such as the stain of green paint in *All Quiet on the Orient Express* – but never seem to lead anywhere or mean anything.

Novelists should probably use MacGuffins with caution, since a plot full of MacGuffins would tend towards the bizarre. But if you're totally stuck for a plot idea, try throwing one in. It might lead you in some strange and interesting directions.

45.
DON'T REVERSE THE POLARITY OF THE NEUTRON FLOW

Any lover of the *Doctor Who* series will recognize the moment when the Doctor, in a tight spot with the Daleks, invokes some new law of nature to save the day. He takes an ordinary-looking hairdryer, and by reversing the polarity of the neutron flow, turns it into a laser; or he summons up a wormhole in time just at the last moment. We accept such things because we love *Doctor Who*, but in novels they should, if possible, be avoided.

Such plot twists are common in the work of writers beginning to explore their craft. They are sometimes called deus ex machina endings. The name translates as 'god from the machine', and comes from the moment in Greek drama when an actor dressed as a god would descend onto the stage in a special mechanical cradle, dispensing justice, rewarding the innocent and punishing the guilty, and tying up all the loose ends.

What's wrong with this? Well, as in the Doctor Who scenario, a deus ex machina ending is extraneous. It doesn't follow on from anything that has happened in the plot so far; it is merely tacked on to get the protagonists out of a tight corner. The result is that the reader feels cheated. Imagine a novel about the struggles of a poor family which ends with some startling coincidence, such as a family member winning the lottery. Or one in which an evil mafia boss, who has been plaguing the neighbourhood for years, dies suddenly on an exercise bike, leaving everyone free to pursue their lives without fear. These plot endings would be totally unacceptable, not so much because these things don't happen in real life, but because they wouldn't show the good guys pooling their resources to get out of their situation. The characters wouldn't need to develop, adapt or change, and this would remove a very healthy chunk of interest from the plot.

Another way of looking at it is to see your novel in terms of conflict (see section 40). If your novel is about a prisoner trying to escape from jail, for example, it won't do for a tree to be blown down and demolish the prison wall just at the right moment. The implied conflict – that of the prisoner against his environment – should instead be resolved in a way that emerges from the prisoner's own efforts. If you set a conflict up, you should allow it to play out. Resolution arrives in the form of a final battle between the protagonist and the forces ranged against him. This way the outcome is meaningful and satisfying.

In short, if your characters are in trouble, don't resolve it with a coincidence, don't invoke some new law of nature, and don't make it all a dream. Readers expect more.

46.
WHAT IF YOU ONLY HAVE SCENES AND NO PLOT?

Writers who are in the early stages of writing a novel often have an idea of their characters, plus a few odd scenes, but no real idea of the plot as a whole. Iris Murdoch, commenting on this sense of dislocation, said: 'The beginning of a novel is a time of awful torment, when you're dealing with a lot of dead pieces and you have to wait and wait for some kind of animation.'

Writers build their novels from very little. As they go, they accumulate research, throw in observations of themselves or others, and try to whip it all into some sort of shape. But what if the shape isn't coming?

The problem is probably in one of two key areas: either it's not clear what your characters want, or there isn't enough conflict.

So firstly, go back and establish what it is your characters want (see section 33). It might be anything, from stopping a dripping tap to saving the world. If this desire only exists in embryo, make it more powerful. Then, crucially, give them obstacles to this desire.

Secondly, remember the possible sources of conflict: inner, inter- and outer (see section 40). Give your characters a believable antagonist – someone who wants them to fail – or some other challenge to which they are forced to react.

Finally, bear in mind that your characters should change by the end of the novel. If you put in dramatic events that don't change the characters or reveal anything much about them, the reader will think: 'all that for nothing?'

47.
WRITE A DETAILED PLOT SUMMARY

Some novelists start writing with a detailed plan in mind. They know everything, from the hero's date of birth to the precise number of bodies that will be left on the floor at the climax.

Other novelists start writing without even knowing what type of book it is (comic, historical, thriller), let alone who will be in it or what will happen at the end. They simply write freely and spontaneously, trusting the muse.

It's difficult for the novice author to know which type of novelist they are, but I would recommend trying the planning approach as well as the free, spontaneous approach. I would like to suggest that the former has some significant advantages.

Firstly, if you plan, you will see exactly how much material you've got and whether it really fits the novel form. In section 37 I generated a plot about an artist who confronts his noisy neighbours and realizes that he doesn't want to go to the Himalayas. It was immediately apparent, once I'd sketched out the plot, that it only gave enough material for a short story. Without planning, I might perhaps have got half-way through the novel before realizing that the structure – indeed, what the novel was fundamentally about – would have to be different.

Secondly, writing a plot summary will give your novel a sense of rhythm and balance. Its parts and acts will be of harmonious proportions. There won't be too many exciting scenes next to one another, for example; they will be separated by scenes of reflection or interludes of some other kind – romantic, perhaps.

Thirdly, if you've planned your novel in advance, you can write the scenes you are interested in when you feel like it, flitting from one part of the book to another, rather than having to approach the plot consecutively. Plotting in advance thus gives a sense of liberation rather than, as one might imagine, a sense of restriction.

Fourthly, you can foreshadow events and build character to make later actions seem plausible.

A plot summary is best written as a table with numbered scenes. You can give an indication of chapters, parts and 'acts' (see the next section). If, as you write, you deviate from the plan, it's no problem. You simply revise the plan. That's the beauty of being an author: you're self-employed.

Planning your novel is rather like drawing up your character CVs (see section 22): it's hard work while you are doing it, but invaluable when you need to remind yourself of what you're trying to achieve.

48.
USE A THREE-ACT STRUCTURE

Dividing a story into three 'acts', or parts, is a strategy widely used in screenwriting. It can also be useful for novelists.

If you think about it, the three-act structure chimes with one of the oldest and most basic ways of telling a story: beginning, middle and end. *The Pied Piper of Hamelin* has three acts: piper lures rats; people refuse to pay; piper takes children. Or *Cinderella*: girl is exploited by sisters; girl goes to ball; prince finds girl. Three acts also reflect the way we think of our lives: youth, middle age and old age; or birth, marriage and death.

In a novel, the first act might give us the main character and her world, and include some crisis or dramatic event that propels her on a journey or quest. The second act might deal with the challenges she meets, and describe the gathering forces that will lead to the final showdown. The third act will give us this showdown, resolving the conflicts and tying up loose ends, with the heroine returning to the place she started from, or, if the book is a tragedy, being defeated at the hands of an antagonist.

Let's take a test case. In *Nineteen Eighty-Four* by George Orwell, the first act establishes Winston Smith's life in Victory Mansions and his job as a functionary of the Outer Party. The second act details his affair and rebellion with Julia. The third gives us his imprisonment and interrogation by O'Brien. Each of these acts is linked to the next by a moment of transition. The transition between the first and second act is Winston's receipt of the note from Julia saying 'I love you'. The transition between the second and the third acts is Winston and Julia's arrest by the Thought Police in Mr Charrington's upstairs bedroom. Each transition propels Winston into the following act, and, importantly, each is irreversible; after each, it is impossible for Winston to return to the previous stasis. A defining moment has been reached that gives the act that follows a separate milieu and character.

Try examining your novel to see if it falls naturally into three acts. Readers feel a powerful sense of identification with this ancient storytelling form.

49.
USE CINEMATIC TECHNIQUES

Do we need more Hollywood in our novels? Perhaps we do. Here are three things that the movies do well that novels often don't:

1. They emphasize scenes. In films, there is a new scene every time we switch to a new location or a new character. Movie scenes are typically short – sometimes only a few seconds, and rarely longer than a few minutes. This keeps the film flowing quickly, maintaining the level of interest. Film scenes are usually very efficient. They try hard to build character, develop the plot, or give essential information. Remembering these important aspects of cinematic scene-writing can act as a useful corrective to novelistic prose that is long-winded, shapeless or aimless.

2. They foreground action and dialogue over thoughts, exposition and description (for a discussion of the five modes of storytelling, see section 58 onwards). Film is a visual and aural medium, after all, so it could hardly be otherwise. But many novelists could learn from the very restrictiveness of film, since the temptation in novels is often to show the thoughts and memories of characters, or to describe the physical environment in a generalized manner, or to explain backstory, simply because novelists can. It's not always the right choice. Robert Louis Stevenson said: 'No human being ever spoke of scenery for above two minutes at a time, which makes me suspect that we hear too much of it in literature.' If you concentrate too much on thoughts, memories and descriptions – weather both meteorological and psychic – you are likely to lose energy and pace in your storytelling.

3. Screenwriters try to elicit powerful emotion. They often move their audiences to tears of laughter or sadness, not because they have the luxury of being able to exploit huge images and surround-sound, but because they've made strong emotion a priority. Novelists would do well to imitate this (see section 84 for a discussion of the importance of emotional content). A novel that is emotionally uninvolving is rarely memorable.

You may disagree with these points, of course. You may feel that the rollercoaster ride of a Hollywood blockbuster is an inappropriate model to use for a novel, and that novels should be more thoughtful, more considered, more subtle. There's some truth in this: a novel is not a film, and novels have their own unique virtues. But screenwriters work very hard to make sure moviegoers don't walk out of the cinema; novelists should work just as hard to make sure readers don't put down a book.

50.
ADD A SUBPLOT

So far I've spoken of plot in the singular. But a novel may have more than one plot running at once. There may be a main plot, and one or more subplots.

Their most important function of a subplot is to provide variety. Short novels can survive with just one main narrative thread: think of JD Salinger's *The Catcher in The Rye* or Saul Bellow's *Seize the Day*. These novels are able to follow a single main character without any danger of boredom. But in long novels, if all we ever do is follow the struggles of the main character for page after page, monotony can creep in. In a longer novel the reader begins to desire something new, a new perspective, even a new narrative point of view; that's the reason long novels often use some variant of the third person that lets readers look into the heads of different characters at different times.

Subplots can also add narrative suspense. In John Kennedy Toole's *A Confederacy of Dunces*, we are mainly interested in the progress of the hero, Ignatius J Reilly; but we are also treated to episodes in the home-lives of numerous other minor characters. These have the effect of delaying the main narrative, and when we come back to Ignatius, it is with a feeling of pleasurable anticipation. We are ready to take up the plot-threads that were left dangling when we last heard from him.

The subplot will almost always be linked to the main plot, but will have its own interest. It will probably spin off from one of the secondary characters (see the concept of character tiers in section 23). In *Persuasion* by Jane Austen, for example, we have the character of the heroine's friend, Mrs Smith, living in straitened circumstances in Bath. Her plight forms a subplot, and it is finally resolved when Captain Wentworth, the heroine's fiancé, intervenes on her behalf. Here we see another important aspect of the subplot: it can echo the main theme. So where the heroine, Anne, is concerned about the 'persuasion' brought to bear on her by her relatives, Mrs Smith has also been a victim of the 'persuasion' of William Elliot.

One possibility is that, as you write, you will find yourself more and more attracted to your subplot, until finally it takes over. Don't necessarily resist this. Your subplot, by mounting a hostile takeover bid, is trying to tell you something important: your main plot is not strong enough. In the early stages of writing a novel, it's quite common for the main plot and the subplot to switch places.

THE MATTER OF STRUCTURE

51.
CRAFT A GOOD BEGINNING

There are many ways to begin a novel, and no single one of them is right. There is, however, one thing the writer would be foolish to ignore. The beginning should make the reader want to read on. It should hook them and make them reluctant to put the book down.

So how can this be done?

One good way is to think about character. Novels are about characters (see section 24 onwards). You won't be going far wrong if you introduce a well-drawn and compelling character as early as possible – on the first page.

Characters in themselves are static, though. They should be shown acting, responding in some way. The opening of your novel will benefit greatly from a sense of conflict and movement. Something should happen to the character to propel them into the plot. Something abnormal, outside the realm of their day-to-day life (as far as you have established it): a death, a journey, a challenge, a discovery, a surprise, a significant meeting. It may be that this abnormal event is something that's been in your mind's eye ever since you started thinking about the book. This event may also introduce suspense: what will happen next?

Some examples. Your character might be an aspiring politician. The situation you put her in might be sitting on a train next to an environmental activist. Plenty of opportunity for an interesting beginning there. Or your character might be a man who doesn't know how offensive his body odour is. What to do with him? Give him a date with someone he's just met on the internet, of course.

At this point it's a good idea to take a step back and ask yourself, once more – what is your novel trying to say? In other words, what is its theme (section 15): the thing that that gives the book life beyond itself? Look at the opening scene you've sketched out. Is that theme there right from the beginning? If your opening scene is the politician and the eco-warrior on the train, and your theme is 'Money makes the world go round', then how does your opening scene reflect the theme? Is one of the characters caught fare-dodging, or with the wrong ticket? The reason to incorporate the theme as early as possible is that if you do, the reader will immediately be immersed in what might be described (a little ostentatiously) as the moral universe of your book. It will immediately be clear what your book is trying to say.

So, three good ingredients for a compelling beginning: character, movement and theme.

52.
CRAFT A BEGINNING THAT ISN'T REALLY A BEGINNING

The traditional novel – by which I mean novels written in the eighteenth and nineteenth centuries – tended to begin at a point rather a long way from their own main events, and thus rather a long way from the action and movement I talked about in the last couple of pages. They tended to begin, in fact, with the childhood, boyhood and youth of the main character, incorporating any number of dull details until the actual plot was permitted to start. The reason is not hard to find: the novel had developed from the biography (which is why early novels are often named after the main character – *Robinson Crusoe, Tom Jones, Pamela,* etc.), and authors were struggling to free themselves from its influence. The practice was parodied pretty much right at the start by Lawrence Sterne in *The Life and Opinions of Tristram Shandy,* in which he described, at some length, the hero's conception. Nowadays, starting with the hero's conception is a very uncommon strategy. But it's still possible to begin with a beginning that isn't really at the inception of the plot. One case in point is the prologue.

A prologue may be set a long time before, or a long time after, the beginning of the story. If the former, it might give an exciting hint of events to come; if the latter, it might include events to which we shall later return. If the book is about a series of murders, for example, the book might start with an excerpt from one of the murders ('The last thing Emmy-Lee remembered was the spider pattern on his gloved hand.') If the prologue includes events that the story must justify, it acts as a potent form of suspense. Prologues are often used in genre fiction: in literary fiction they might seem a little too much like the foregrounding of an authorial trick – but that's a matter of taste.

After the excitement of the prologue, the author is justified in kicking back to some extent in the real opening, even including a little exposition. ('Lawyer Jed Harris reclined in his expensive penthouse apartment and reflected on the day's events.')

Or you can begin with the end. This is not as impossible as it might sound. Most novels begin, in a sense, at the end, since they are being recounted by someone who is speaking at a time after everything in the novel has already happened. More specifically, a novel might begin in a particular place, such as a prison or a desert island, and the author might establish this local scene before saying: 'This is how I got here.'

Either way, your options at the beginning of the book aren't as restricted as you might think.

53.
WRITE THE FIRST SENTENCE

I hope that the preceding two sections have given you some ideas about beginning a novel. So, just for fun, let's try something.

Sitting in front of a keyboard or notebook in a relaxed posture, write the first sentence of your novel.

The strong character need not appear in it; nor any immediate movement; nor any theme. The function of the first sentence is to make the reader want to read the second sentence (and the third, and the fourth). It is to induce curiosity. Who wouldn't want to read the second sentence after reading one of these first sentences:

Of the three men at the table, all dressed in black business suits, two must have been stone drunk.

It was a pleasure to burn.

In the town there were two mutes, and they were always together.

These are the opening lines respectively of *Tunc* by Lawrence Durrell, *Fahrenheit 451* by Ray Bradbury and *The Heart is a Lonely Hunter* by Carson McCullers. The reader wants to know:

Why were two drunk and the third not?
Burn what?
What's this about two mutes?

The first sentence introduces a question. The rest of the novel answers it.

54.
STRUGGLE THROUGH THE MIDDLE

The traditional division of a story is into beginning, middle and end. But of the three, the middle is the odd one out. The beginning sets the scene, introduces the characters and hooks the reader's interest. The end ties everything up, resolves the conflicts, and bids the reader goodbye. Both beginning and end have specific jobs to do. In comparison, what is the middle? It's amorphous. It has no agreed function or shape.

This is partly what makes middles so difficult to write. But there's another problem. From the point of view of the writer, the beginning is the honeymoon, in which the novel still excites them; they can't wait to unzip their file in the morning and get to work. But when the first few weeks, say, of writing are over, the thrill has gone. There is so much to do: the novel stretches out forever, the characters begin to turn to sludge. This is where a lot of writers give up: at around the 10,000 word mark.

These two problems compound one another. If you're confronted with the task of writing something amorphous, at a time when you're losing interest anyway, the pressure on you to stop is all but irresistible.

The solution is to tackle each problem independently. The first is the matter of structure. A middle is shapeless, yes, until you give it a shape. This is where planning comes in. Write a detailed plot summary (see section 47). Ask yourself these questions: what obstacles have you prepared for the characters, so as to drive the plot? Are your subplots developed at the level of detail they need to be? Your character should change by the end of the book: have you prepared adequately for this? Will the change seem believable when it comes? Have aspects of the climax been foreshadowed? Is there suspense? Is there a believable antagonist? There's actually a lot to do in the middle. Don't go into it hoping it will just happen: plan it out.

The second problem is the matter of a loss of authorial drive. There is only one cure for this: grit your teeth and keep going. Keep reaching your word- or your time-target (see section 8), even if you hate it. As the pages accumulate, the excitement you first felt will begin slowly to build back up. Finally it will be as good as anything you felt at the beginning: better, even. By the time you have pushed through the middle and can see the end in sight, your whole conception of yourself as a writer will be different. You will no longer see yourself as a mere sprinter; instead, you will see yourself as a marathon runner. And, if you get through the middle, this is what exactly what you will be. A novel is essentially a distance event.

55.

CLIMAX OR DENOUEMENT?

Beginning, middle, end. What a reassuring triad. And readers who have been regaled with a beginning and a middle want an end – a good one, one that satisfies.

I've already talked about resolutions (see section 42). For a resolution to occur – that is, for all the forces in the book to dissipate and settle back into a new stasis – you need a climax. The climax is where the tensions and conflicts of the plot build to a head and explode. For example, if your book is about the conflict between a hero and an antagonist, the pair must have their final showdown. If the heroine is on a quest, she must find the thing she has been looking for (and possibly be presented with something she wasn't expecting). If the novel is about a man with three secret lovers, those lovers should all find out about each other. Imagine if these things didn't happen: if the hero and the antagonist kissed and made up, if the heroine decided the quest wasn't worth the candle, if the man was never faced with the consequences of his secret life. The result would be bitter disappointment. The conflicts of the plot would never detonate: it would be like a sneeze that gets half way and stalls in your nose.

In brief, then, the climax is the logical outworking of the beginning and the middle. Remember, it should not involve a 'deus ex machina' twist – no sudden rescues, convenient deaths, or lottery jackpots. It should be a working-out of the characters' personalities and actions.

And then, after the climax, comes (at least traditionally) the denouement. Denouement is a French word meaning 'untying' or 'unravelling'. You will recognize it from any Shakespeare tragedy. After the last body has fallen to the floor, there is one remaining character who makes a final speech, commenting on the grisly waste of life and speculating on what it all means. In prose fiction we see it in the Sherlock Holmes stories, where, after the excitement of the climax, Watson gives us a couple of paragraphs beginning with something such as: 'And that was the end of the case of the Woman with the Twisted Ear. She went to British Columbia and married a fur trapper.' In fact, Mark Twain referred to the denouement as 'the marryin' and the buryin'' phase of the novel.

In twentieth-century fiction, especially literary fiction, there has been a tendency away from the neat tying up of loose ends. If your novel is more about an emotional journey or an inner change, there doesn't need to be as explosive a climax, or as neat a tie-up at the end. But there should still be a sense of ending and some sense of reflection, or of going forward into the future.

56.
WRITE THE LAST SENTENCE

Charles Reade was perhaps the quintessential Victorian novelist, fantastically successful in his day, now fantastically unread. His novels all end in the same way: moralistically, usually with a description of the hero or heroine's virtuous death. The last sentence of *Peg Woffington* reads:

> When the great summons came, it found her full of hope, and peace, and joy; sojourning, not dwelling, upon earth; far from dust and din and vice; the Bible in her hand, the Cross in her heart; quiet; amid grass, and flowers, and charitable deeds.

Victorian novelists loved closure, and death is the ultimate closure. But there were Victorian rebels too. Henry James disparaged endings that were 'a distribution at the last of prizes, pensions, husbands, wives, babies, millions, appended paragraphs, and cheerful remarks'. Samuel Butler ended *Erewhon*, surprisingly, in the middle of things:

> At the last moment I see a probability of a complication which causes me much uneasiness.

Please subscribe quickly. Address to the Mansion-House, care of the Lord Mayor, whom I will instruct to receive names and subscriptions for me until I can organise a committee.

The twentieth century followed this pattern, shying away from moralistic, highly-resolved last sentences, and instead presenting final lines that were open-ended, sometimes subtly evoking a theme. *Something Happened* by Joseph Heller ends with the sentence:

Everyone seems pleased with the way I've taken command.

This is highly ironic because the main character has just 'taken command' by mistakenly smothering his son to death, and the theme of the novel is that of a man who has failed to take command of his life. Other modern novels end with a scrap of dialogue. Bernard Malamud's *A New Life* ends with the words of a keen photographer (a husband whose wife the main character has stolen):

'Got your picture!'

Others end with a journey to a new place, or an offhand authorial remark, suggesting that the reader is free to continue the book as they wish. These sorts of last sentences do not focus inward on the book and obtain closure of its fictional world, but look outward, suggesting that the world of the book goes on.

57.
SPLIT YOUR NOVEL INTO CHAPTERS

Why are novels split into pieces? One might blame nineteenth-century serialization, but for the fact that novelists were doing this in the eighteenth century when novels were intended to be read straight through. The major influence was probably biography – we still speak of the 'chapters' of a person's life – and, earlier, classical texts and the Bible that had been split into manageable chunks for ease of reference. Whatever their origins, chapters serve a variety of functions in novels. A new chapter can signal a jump forwards or backwards in time. It can signal a jump sideways in space. It can also be a sort of literary palate-cleansing exercise, conveying a new start or new way of looking at things.

And there is no doubt that chapters make a book easier to read. Dense, unbroken text that seems to stretch on forever with no break, through which it is impossible to navigate – to find where you left off reading, to skip forward to something more interesting, or to locate a favourite part on re-reading – is likely to be significantly more taxing on the reader.

How many chapters? It's entirely a matter of taste. Novelists enjoy playing with chapters, as well as with the clusters of chapters known as 'parts' (Part I, Part II), to give a novel an overall architecture and symmetry. Anthony Burgess particularly enjoyed this aspect of novel-writing, and divided each of the three parts of *A Clockwork Orange* into seven chapters, adding up to twenty-one in all, twenty-one being (so he said) the age at which a young person achieves adult maturity.

TYPES OF PROSE WRITING

58.
GIVE EXPOSITION – SPARINGLY

There are five main modes of storytelling. They are: exposition, description, action, dialogue and thoughts.

The first, exposition, is explanation of how a given situation came to be. It takes place 'behind' the story; it gives background. Exposition can occur at the beginning of a novel, to set the scene, or at any point during the novel. Information given by the narrator about a character's childhood, or their job, or why they collect antique telephones, is exposition. Sometimes the information is essential to the story. Often, though, it can actually get in the way of the story.

The reason for this is that exposition isn't inherently dramatic. There's little action in facts, or in giving explanations and clarifications. The energy level of the story drops.

Here's an innocent-looking piece of exposition:

Sarah hadn't wanted to come to the party, but Michael, who wanted to cultivate the Fosters, had insisted.

This is exposition – it gives background. It provides the reader with two snippets of information: Sarah hadn't wanted to come to the party and Michael wanted to cultivate the Fosters. It doesn't give us the chance to read between the lines, and we don't participate in any discovery – it's handed to us on a plate. Of course, it's useful to know. But it can be shown in other ways – for example in dialogue.

> 'Are you ready?' asked Michael. 'Foster said we ought to aim for eight thirty. I don't want to be late.'
> 'Ready as I'll ever be,' said Sarah.

Or in action:

> Michael pushed her into the car. Later she felt her arm. There was a bruise.

It is possible, naturally, to get away with exposition, but it's best to be aware of the alternatives; and most stories can survive with a minimum of background. We don't always need to know everything. We don't need to know about Hercule Poirot's childhood in Belgium, and what infantile traumas led him to become a detective. Exposition can often seem like 'too much information'.

Even if you do give exposition, don't always give it straight away – withhold it. The withholding of exposition is a form of suspense, and suspense keeps readers turning pages.

59.
DESCRIBE THINGS

Description is the second narrative mode. It gives information about people, things and places ('She was tall and blonde with a mouth shaped like a keyhole...' 'My socks stank to high heaven...' 'The cottage was of rose with stones round the door...' etc.). Description happens as the story is happening, in the 'story plane'. If you say 'the coins lay in golden heaps, dazzling to the eye,' the details of the coins are in the time-frame of the story, despite being in the past tense, and therefore count as description. If, on the other hand, you say 'the coins had been collected by his uncle the third earl of Mountfitchet', you are going further into the past, into background time, and giving exposition (see the preceding section).

Description doesn't have quite the same bad rap as exposition. However, not all description is equal. If you describe a person by saying 'He was greedy,' you are making the same mistake as you might in exposition. If you describe the same person through action, showing them acting greedily, you gain vividness (see the following section for examples).

Good descriptions are wedded to the senses. We all share human bodies, yet we label intense physical experiences 'personal'. In fact they are nothing of the sort: they are communal. When a writer describes one of these experiences, we receive a shock of recognition.

Description need not appeal only to the senses; it may ramify outwards to include the psyche. Proust's madeleine is a case in point. He bit into the cake, yes – but the experience went much further than taste: it conjured up a whole childhood. The senses are gateways to emotions and memories. If you describe something, don't forget to consider a further option beyond the sensual: how it made your character feel.

60.
LET YOUR CHARACTERS ACT

Action is the third main narrative mode. Action is distinguished by things happening.

By 'action' I don't mean the kind of action that you get in thrillers. I mean action in a more technical sense. If the heroine is fighting a tiger in a crippled helicopter, that is certainly action, but it is also action if the hero allows his fingers to trail languidly over a tiger-skin rug. What counts is that the character (or an inanimate object such as a machine or a landscape) does something: an active verb is involved.

As we saw in section 91, it's possible to introduce a character by having them do something. If a character is shown acting, there is immediate interest in that character, and often immediate drama. There is also often immediate suspense. Actions may have consequences that the reader can only learn about by turning the page. And if there is one thing that the author should want his readers to do, more than anything else, it is turn the page.

Action is the one mode of narrative that best follows

the 'show, don't tell' rule. This rule means that it is better to allow your readers to discover things for themselves rather than lecture them about it. There is a lot of difference between 'Clarence was an ambitious man' and 'Clarence strode into the reception area, slammed his CV on the desk, and said: "Call me."' In the first example we are being presented with information. In the second we are shown a real human being. We want to know whether Clarence gets anywhere with this tactic. The fundamental difference is that in the second example we see that Clarence is ambitious. In the first we're merely informed that he is.

Action is concrete. As an author, you may wish to convey that your heroine is petite. Don't say 'she's petite'; say that when she came to answer the door, her shadow behind the frosted glass fooled the caller into thinking it was a child answering the bell. Or you may wish to convey that your character is careful with money. Don't say it outright; say: 'He picked it up, turned it over judiciously and put it back in the box marked "five pence each".'

Exposition, description, dialogue and thoughts, all have their place; but it is through the use of active verbs, things happening, that you will often produce your most engaging and involving prose.

61.
MAKE YOUR DIALOGUE WORK

First of all, the mechanics.

Dialogue can be presented in a number of different ways, but in modern novels, dialogue is generally put in single quote marks. If needed you can then put double quote marks within the single ('I've never tried "Gak" before,' Brady said. 'What is it?')

Every time a new character speaks, they have a new line. But actions associated with a character are usually in the same paragraph. ('I've never tried "Gak" before,' Brady said. He stroked his small beard. 'What is it?')

You can use attributive verbs instead of 'said', but be careful not to overdo them. Anything more complicated and you tend to wind up sounding like Conan Doyle: 'It was a confession,' I ejaculated.

This also goes for expostulated, exclaimed, hesitated, proffered, sniped, muttered, interjected, retorted. Used sparingly, they are effective ('"Reginald!" she brayed.'; '"Be more assertive," he whispered.') Used redundantly, they are ridiculous.

Second of all, the function of dialogue. What is your dialogue doing? In novels, unlike in real life, there is a story, and a story involves a) plot and b) characters. Dialogue should contribute to the development of the plot or the characters, or it will risk seeming irrelevant, and may even confuse the reader, who will think 'Why is this in here? Have I missed something?'

However, it gets more complicated. If you give too much plot or character information in your dialogue, it will read very much like exposition (see section 58). Imagine two speakers who say things like: "'I remember – you were working in Tesco's, weren't you..." "Yes and that's where I met James..." "Did James ever survive that fall from the cliff?..." "Yes, his fall was broken by that beached whale...'"

The secret lies in that old screenwriting tip: 'Don't write on the nose'. Give information, but subtly. Don't let the characters say what they really think. People bend the truth, cover up, make excuses, present things in a way favourable to them. Let the readers work out for themselves what's really going on. If you trust your readers to guess what your characters mean, the readers will be able to participate in the gradually unfolding drama, much as we all do in real life, where we have to fill in the gaps and ferret into motivations.

Finally, a trick. Speak your dialogue aloud. You will soon notice any false notes.

62.
ATTRIBUTE YOUR DIALOGUE – OR DON'T

When writing dialogue we use subject markers such as 'he said' or 'she said' (and occasionally 'he ejaculated' or 'she ejaculated'). However these can be dispensed with if the characters are strong enough – that is, if their speech patterns are recognizable enough for them not to need marking.

Have a look at this:

'Do you need anything?' asked Jennifer.

'Apart from a bloody miracle, no,' Colin replied.

'Oh come on,' said Jennifer. She sat on the bed. 'You're doing fine.'

'They're going to take my leg off,' said Colin. 'How is that fine?'

'We don't know that for sure.'

'We bloody do.'

'Come on, now.'

'Christ, it's killing me.'

'Just try and get some sleep.'

'I'd like to see you bloody sleep with gangrene in your leg.'
'We don't know for sure its gangrene.'
'Why is it green then?'
'It might be just a normal part of the healing process.'
'Healing process my arse.'

This is a rather silly piece of dialogue, but the point is that in the last ten lines there is no indication of who is speaking; yet we are sure nevertheless who is saying what.

Try writing a similar piece of dialogue featuring Colin and Jennifer, in any situation they may find themselves in. The first four lines should be attributed, but the following ten unattributed. If there is a strong enough sense of who Colin is and who Jennifer is, the reader should be able to get to the end without confusion.

63.
USE DIALECT?

How far should you attempt to reproduce the way people actually speak? In his Nottinghamshire stories DH Lawrence went about as far as he could. Here is an extract from his short story 'Odour of Chrysanthemums':

> There was another pause. Rigley had evidently something to get off his mind: 'Ah left 'im finishin' a stint,' he began. 'Loose-all 'ad bin gone about ten minutes when we com'n away, an' I shouted, "Are ter comin', Walt?" an' 'e said, "Go on, Ah shanna be but a'ef a minnit," so we com'n ter th' bottom, me an' Bowers, thinkin' as 'e wor just behint, an' 'ud come up i' th' next bantle – '

Lawrence had a point to make: he wanted to put working people's voices at the heart of serious literature. But sometimes it's as if he's writing a crib sheet for Martians. And is it not perhaps a little counterproductive? It's a small step from suggesting that someone doesn't speak standard English (DH Lawrence didn't write the 'narrator' passages in dialect after all) to suggesting that they are uneducated, and from there that they are unsophisticated, and from there that they are ignorant, and from there that they are laughable. Any writer who attempts to represent dialect speech runs this dangerous gamut. If you write 'somefinks up wivvit' instead of 'something's up with it', are you covertly making a point about the intellectual capacities of Londoners? Unless you are very sure of your ground you will seem patronizing. There are exceptions, of course: we trust Lawrence's motives, even if his dialect is occasionally wearing.

The truth is, of course, that none of us speaks in such a way as to mirror written English. A 'Received Pronunciation' English speaker wouldn't say (as in the first sentence of the Lawrence extract above) 'There was another pause' but something like 'Theh wuz anutha paws'.

It's safest, then, to treat dialect with caution. In any case, there are other choices available. You can suggest a particular manner of speech by sentence construction, for example. A Japanese person speaking English will often begin sentences with the grammatical topic, which translates to 'As for...' ('As for holidays, I prefer Europe.') In a historical novel, a speaker might use many more subordinate clauses than a modern speaker would, though might still keep to an essentially modern vocabulary. These sorts of tricks enable you to give a flavour of speech without having either to reproduce it quasi-phonetically or to throw in handfuls of baffling dialect words.

64.
SHOW MINDS AT WORK

The fifth and final mode of narrative is the showing of thoughts: people considering, observing, pondering, wondering, remembering.

The most obvious way to show people's thoughts is in a first-person narrative. Here the narrator lets us into his own mind, giving us a privileged insight. The narrator shows what he thinks and feels as he tries to get to grips with the world. Sometimes there will be an opposition between what the narrator thinks and what he says, or between what he thinks and what he does, which can be amusing or ironic. Willem Elsschot's *Cheese* is full of such moments:

> 'Don't you want to try a bit?' my wife finally asked, having swallowed a couple of pieces. 'It's really tasty.'
>
> I don't like cheese, but what else could I do? Shouldn't I set an example from now on? Shouldn't I lead the army of cheese-eaters from the front?

Thoughts can just as easily appear in a third person narrative. In fact, third-person thoughts have a special believability. The first person narrator may have any number of reasons for presenting his thoughts, opinions and ideas in a certain way: to cast a more flattering light on himself, for instance. A novelist writing in the third person, on the other hand, has no reason to deceive the reader when it comes to his characters' thoughts. The thoughts of his characters are as much a statement of 'fact' as descriptions of their appearance or speech.

In the modernist writing of the early twentieth century there was a new development in the presentation of thoughts. This was the 'internal monologue' or 'stream-of-consciousness' style (the two terms are often considered separately but they refer essentially to the same thing). Here the author mimics the way mental events happen: that is, the way one thought emerges, displaces another and is succeeded by yet another, sometimes in a subtle pattern of cause and effect but perhaps also irrelevantly and illogically. And this encompasses not simply conscious thoughts: in novels such as James Joyce's *Ulysses* or Virginia Woolf's *To the Lighthouse* we are often presented with half-acknowledged, subconscious or unconscious thoughts. By investigating the nature of mental processes in this way, modernist writers made thinking itself part of the subject of novels.

65.
USE LETTERS

In the eighteenth century, at the birth of the novel, it was considered quite acceptable to tell a story exclusively in the form of letters. Novels using this strategy are known as 'epistolary novels'. *Pamela* (1740) and *Clarissa* (1748) by Samuel Richardson are two examples; both were colossal Europe-wide bestsellers. *Shamela* (1741) by Henry Fielding mocked Pamela and some of the absurdities of the form (such as a woman writing five letters on her wedding night). The fashion was also prevalent on the Continent, with examples including Goethe's highly influential *The Sorrows of Young Werther* (1774).

Nevertheless, the approach fell out of favour in the nineteenth century, and the epistolary form was relegated to the attic of novelistic devices. In the twentieth century, novels composed entirely of letters were uncommon (*The Color Purple* by Toni Morrison being an exception).

This is perhaps a shame, since the use of letters brings numerous advantages. As documents, they have a certain authority, appearing to present the action as it really happened, and so can simulate 'real life'. They give multiple viewpoints: you can include letters from numerous different characters, each recounting the same events in a different way (sometimes a very different way). They lend themselves very well to comic effect, as Fielding showed in *Shamela*. And they are great plot generators. If you're stuck for an idea, have the protagonist receive a letter. It could get your book moving in an unexpected new direction.

Or perhaps, if your characters don't so readily employ a pen and paper, try the modern successors to the letter: the email, the text, the tweet, the blog and the social network post. Entire novels have already been created exclusively from these things.

66.
TRY A DIARY-NOVEL

What about a novel in the form of a diary? It's a time-honoured strategy. It might be argued, in fact, that the novel grew partly out of the diary in the eighteenth century. Certainly, early novels modelled themselves on existing literary forms, and if the biography gave rise to the third-person narrative, and the letter to the epistolary novel, it is tempting to see the diary as giving rise to the first-person narrative. But the first fictions that explicitly presented themselves as diaries came about in the nineteenth century. Examples include Nikolai Gogol's 'Diary of a Madman' and George Grossmith's *Diary of a Nobody*; they later developed into twentieth-century diary-novels such as William Golding's *Rites of Passage* or Helen Fielding's *Bridget Jones's Diary*.

There are also novels which include snippets of diaries amid the main narrative. About a fifth of Graham Greene's *The End of the Affair* is written in the form of diary entries, and Albert Camus' *The Plague* incorporates the diary entries of one character, Tarrou.

What are the advantages of the diary form? Like the first-person narrative, it can showcase a distinctive voice (see section 70). There may be strong elements of an unreliable narrator (section 71), one who conceals certain things or reveals much more about themselves than they intend (for example Sue Townsend's *The Secret Diary of Adrian Mole Aged 13¾*). A diary-novel is addressed essentially to the diarist himself, making it the ultimate 'intimate' form; a first-person narrative, by contrast, has an implicit or explicit addressee to whom the narrator wishes to tell a story.

There is a strong potential for comedy in the diary-novel. Some of the greatest diary-novels chart the day-to-day struggles of unremarkable people as they try to cope with employers, girlfriends, boyfriends, and other slings and arrows of outrageous fortune. Each day brings more humiliation, demonstrating the essential human truth that any life examined with complete honesty from the inside is merely a series of disasters.

Other diary-novels are darker: they chart the spiral of the diarist into despair or insanity, each entry being more deranged than the last. The diary-novel in this case is an opportunity for some virtuoso first-person writing. Not only do you have to create a convincing narrator, but adapt the narrator's voice as their personality begins to disintegrate.

67.

STEAL FROM THE THEATRE

So far I've mentioned letters and diaries as alternative formal possibilities. But if you think about it, there are a number of other forms you can integrate into your novel.

Some novels, for example, suddenly turn into plays. George Orwell's *A Clergyman's Daughter* is an example: in Chapter Three, as Orwell's heroine Dorothy is forced to sleep rough in London, the text slips into dramatic mode.

> [SCENE: Trafalgar Square. Dimly visible through the mist, a dozen people, Dorothy among them, are grouped about one of the benches near the north parapet.]
> CHARLIE [singing]: 'Ail Mary, 'ail Mary, 'a-il Ma-ary – [Big Ben strikes ten.]
> SNOUTER [mimicking the noise]: Ding dong, ding dong! Shut your – noise, can't you? Seven more hours of it on this – square before we get the chance of a setdown and a bit of sleep! Cripes!

Anthony Burgess, as part of his novel *The Clockwork Testament*, includes several pages of a screenplay, as well as a tape-transcript of a TV show. Lewis Carroll in the Alice books includes poems and songs. Chapter Five of *Post Office* by Charles Bukowski is made up entirely of warning letters from his employer. William Burroughs in *Naked Lunch* includes text from menus:

> Filet of Sun-Ripened Sting Ray basted with Eau de Cologne and garnished with nettles.
> The After-Birth Supreme de Boeuf, cooked in drained crank case oil served with a piquant sauce of rotten egg-yolks and crushed bed-bugs.

I've already mentioned emails, tweets, blog posts and so on. Other forms you might use might include: trial transcripts, advertisements, invented encyclopaedia entries, newspaper articles, quotations from foreign texts or mysterious inscriptions, railway timetables, course curricula, government reports, how-to guide extracts... In fact, the whole gamut of the world of writing is there for you to plunder.

The point is that you don't need to restrict yourself to conventional modes of narration. No holds are barred. Even if only as short excerpts, you can include all sorts of other media. These may liberate you imaginatively as well as providing your readers with a more interesting and entertaining reading experience.

68.
WRITE WITH PICTURES

And the final type of 'discourse' you can use is not even literary at all.

Many novelists have worked with pictures. Dickens was illustrated by Hablot Knight Browne ('Phiz'); Conan Doyle by Sidney Paget. In the twentieth century it became less common for novels to be accompanied by drawings, but there were exceptions (*Fear and Loathing in Las Vegas* by Hunter S Thompson, for example, with illustrations by Ralph Steadman). And novelists began illustrating their own work. Mervyn Peake produced the illustrations for his *Gormenghast* trilogy; Kurt Vonnegut in *Breakfast of Champions* included numerous line drawings, of, among other things, his own rear end; Toby Litt in *Adventures in Capitalism* included graphic representations of lapel badges; and there are many more examples.

It lies outside the scope of this book, but it is possible, of course, to write an entire novel in pictures – the so-called 'graphic novel'. The form is still young, but it has already had some outstanding exponents and shows no sign of going away. Will Eisner's *A Contract with God* is an exploration of the lives of ordinary people in a Bronx tenement; *Maus* by Art Spiegelman is an extraordinary Holocaust memoir; *Logicomix* by Apostolos Doxiadis and Christos Papadimitriou is a complex narrative concerning Alfred North Whitehead and Bertrand Russell's *Principia Mathematica*. The late Harvey Pekar is another fascinating figure: he wrote stories of American life which were then illustrated by a range of artists including Robert Crumb and Dean Haspiel, and produced a 'graphic autobiography', *The Quitter*. So if your talent lies in a pictorial direction, don't rule it out as a possibility.

POINT OF VIEW

69.
GET TO GRIPS WITH POINT OF VIEW

In fiction, point of view (also known as viewpoint) refers to the particular narrative angle from which things are presented. If you use the pronoun 'I' (I did this, I did that) you are using the first person point of view. If you use the pronouns 'he' and 'she' (he did this, she did that), you are using the third person point of view.

So, to clarify, point of view in fiction does not have the conventional meaning of 'opinion'. It is not the author's particular take on a topic. Nor is it anything to do with the place or time in which the novel is set. It has a purely technical meaning to do with the dominant pronoun used by the narrator.

This seems simple enough, but complications immediately set in. Some books on writing give three main types of point of view. Some give four. Others give five, seven or nine. In fact, there is no general agreement about how many points of view there are, or how finely the various types may be divided.

In this guide I would like to stick my neck out and say that there are two main useful points of view for the novelist: first person and third person. First person is comparatively straightforward, but third person can be further divided into third person limited, third person unlimited and 'God's eye view'. I will discuss each of these in the ensuing sections.

Point of view is an important choice for a writer because each point of view offers opportunities, and writers who can exploit these opportunities put themselves ahead of the game. For example, in the first person point of view there is a golden opportunity to develop the narrator's 'voice': to make the narrator a unique and entertaining character whose way of looking at the world adds a great deal to the reader's enjoyment. Or, in the 'God's eye' view, there is the opportunity to talk about events at which no character could possibly be present – describing, for example, volcanic explosions on Mars.

In fact, point of view colours a novel completely, dictating the reader's experience of the story, its plot and characters, how close we are to them and how distant. It gives the novel its fundamental 'felt life'. David Lodge in *The Art of Fiction* says that choice of point of view is 'arguably the most important single decision that the novelist has to make.'

It's possible to mix and match points of view within the same novel, for example alternating between first and third as in William Faulkner's *The Sound and the Fury*, but this requires a very sure touch. Beginners are well advised to stick to something relatively simple and to understand it thoroughly, getting the most from whatever it can offer.

70.
WRITE IN THE FIRST PERSON

The first person point of view involves an 'I' narrator. It's rather like a diary. I got up, I brushed my teeth – or, if written in the present tense for maximum thrills, I get up, I brush my teeth.

The first person point of view is limited to the narrator's view of life and to the things the narrator chooses to present. If the narrator is reliable, then the narrative will be a more or less honest attempt to tell a story as it 'really happened'. But given the nature of human beings, there will usually be some special pleading. The narrator may even tell outright lies, becoming completely unreliable (see section 71).

First-person writing offers many advantages. It gives readers a single, in-depth, concentrated view, entering fully into a narrator's mind. It is solipsistic: the universe exists for the narrator alone. In a way it is the most natural style of writing, since that is how we all experience reality. It is perhaps not surprising that many writers begin by writing in the first person.

Another important advantage of the first person point of view is that it enables the writer to create a unique voice. Examples are *Moll Flanders* by Daniel Defoe, *Something Happened* by Joseph Heller or *Fight Club* by Chuck Palahniuk. Slang, dialect, ungrammatical sentences, even strange spellings can proliferate. You can write as a period character (*Hawksmoor* by Peter Ackroyd), a teenager (*The Catcher in the Rye* by JD Salinger) or a madman (*One Flew Over the Cuckoo's Nest* by Ken Kesey). First person gives a good platform for the comic novelist, since it can be loaded with irony (the difference between what a character says and what he does, or between how he perceives things and how things evidently are).

One disadvantage of the first person point of view is that information can't be given unless the narrator knows about it. This may restrict plotting to a certain extent. Another, perhaps greater danger, is that the novel may become a little mono-dimensional: the unique voice, especially if it is an irritating or unsympathetic one, may get tiresome, and readers may begin to desire variety. But it is possible to get round this by bringing in a lot of dialogue, or even by having sequential first person narrators, as Tracy Chevalier did in *The Lady and the Unicorn*.

Finally, if you get sick of the first person singular, why not try the first person plural? Jeffrey Eugenides did it very effectively in *The Virgin Suicides*, in which the novel is narrated by a group of boys speaking as a 'we'.

71.
DECIDE WHETHER YOUR NARRATOR IS RELIABLE OR UNRELIABLE

As already mentioned, the narrator of a novel may not be the staunchest upholder of the truth. He or she may even attempt to deceive. The author, who exists behind the narrator, must decide how trustworthy the narrator is going to be.

The phrase 'the unreliable narrator' was coined in 1961 by the literary theorist Wayne C Booth. He wrote: 'I have called a narrator reliable when he speaks for or acts in accordance with the norms of the work (which is to say the implied author's norms), unreliable when he does not.'

The classic case of the unreliable narrator is *The Murder of Roger Ackroyd* by Agatha Christie. The book is narrated in the first person by Dr James Sheppard, but at the end of the book (spoiler here) it turns out that Dr Sheppard is the murderer. All along, as Dr Sheppard has been discussing the slaying, he has been concealing his knowledge of who did it i.e. him.

This is not perhaps the subtlest working-out of the idea, but it makes the point. Narrators may wish to conceal things as well as reveal things. In fact, narrators may conceal things because they are unable to reveal things. There may be some special circumstance that limits or colours their perception of the world. They may be insane, for example, or very young. Sometimes they may be struggling with the truth, trying to reveal it, but never quite managing it. *An Artist of the Floating World* by Kazuo Ishiguro is an example. The book is set in the period following the Second World War, and the first-person narrator is an ageing Japanese artist who has lent his services to the Imperial war machine, and can't face the damage he has done. (Interestingly, Ishiguro pulled off the very same trick in *The Remains of the Day*, also set in the aftermath of the Second World War, in which a butler finds it hard to come to terms with the fact that he has spent his life in service to a traitor.)

The use of an unreliable narrator also lends itself very well to the comic novel. Have a look at this excerpt from the opening of *Augustus Carp, Esq*, by Sir Henry Bashford:

> On every ground I am an unflinching opponent of sin. I have continually rebuked it in others. I have strictly refrained from it in myself. And for that reason alone I have deemed it incumbent upon me to issue this volume.

The reader is not surprised to learn later that the narrator is a ridiculous, bigoted, sanctimonious monster, and the result is comic irony.

72.
WRITE IN THE THIRD PERSON LIMITED

The third person limited point of view is a very common choice for novelists. It's sometimes called the 'over the shoulder' view. Here the author writes in the third person (he did this, she did that), but presents only the thoughts and feelings of one focal character. The thoughts and feelings of the other characters remain a mystery, unless the focal character is sensitive enough to perceive them. The third person limited point of view is therefore very similar to the first person. What are the differences?

For a start, in the third person limited there is a distance between narrator and character, and thus between reader and character. The reader is not asked to identify strongly with the character, which may be a relief if the character is in some way unpleasant or irritating.

Next, 'unreliable narrators' are largely out of the picture. We trust the author – in general – to give us the straight dope on what that character is thinking and feeling.

And finally, the author has the option of introducing an additional focal character to give us an additional perspective – or several additional focal characters. This sort of treatment in fact shades into third person unlimited (see the next section).

The third person limited point of view lends itself naturally to a further development which might be called 'third person voiced' (it's also called the 'free indirect' style). In this type of narration, the author employs aspects of the character's verbal manner in the text itself, or, more radically, veers into out-and-out first person treatment. Consider for example this passage from Brian Moore's *The Lonely Passion of Judith Hearne*, about a Belfast woman struggling with alcoholism:

> She paid and went out. The thought of going back to her room was hateful... It was shameful, shameful. Singing like a crazy woman, lying on the floor of her room, drunken, dirty, sinning, while God in His Heaven looked down at her. And then being forced to humiliate herself in front of a person like Mrs Rice, telling that lie about her monthlies and being caught in it. Could anybody blame her if she despised me? I deserve it. I'm rotten, rotten, just a useless woman, all alone.

The passage starts with 'she' and ends with 'I'. The author has his cake and eats it: he writes in the third person, but uses the intimate vocabulary of his main character ('God in His Heaven', 'monthlies'), even switching mid-paragraph to the first person when he feels like it.

73.
WRITE IN THE THIRD PERSON UNLIMITED

But why stick with third person limited? Why not go all the way?

Third person unlimited is, in a way, the logical development of buried tendencies within third person limited. Many novelists who write in third person limited give in to the temptation, at some point, of introducing a further focal character, for variety. And on the chocolate-box principle ('I'll have just one more'), introduce another – and another, and another, until what they end up with is third person unlimited.

In third person unlimited the author can theoretically inhabit the head of any character, at any time; but in practice there are two essential restrictions. Firstly, the inhabiting is sequential. If it were not, the psychic noise would be like every key on an organ playing at once: cacophony. So if two characters are talking, the well-advised author will stick to the thought-processes of only one character per passage of dialogue. In fact, it's better to separate focal characters by a wide margin: by chapter, or if not, by section-within-chapter.

The second restriction is that despite the word 'unlimited', the third person unlimited will rarely explore the thoughts and feelings of all the characters. Imagine the noisy irrelevance of a novel that entered into the heads of literally everyone who appeared, however minor: ticket-collectors, street-hawkers, people out walking their iguanas. The third-person-unlimited author will ignore the inner lives of the majority, in fact, and allot time to the remaining characters in proportion to their importance to the novel. A good way of looking at this is using the concept of 'character tiers' (see section 23). The most important character is at the top tier of the wedding cake, and is given the most authorial time; the minor characters are on the bottom tier, and are not given any time. Seeing inside the head of every character would be less a wedding cake than a wedding porridge.

Third person limited and third person unlimited are much more difficult to handle than first person. Decisions need constantly to be made about whose perspective to cut to, whether to describe the same scene twice, how quickly to jump-cut between perspectives, how many perspectives are viable in total, who gets the most authorial time, who the least, and who gets the scene if two major characters are in the same scene. But this complexity has the potential to provide a very rich reading experience. If you are bold enough to try it, it's a fascinating way to write a novel.

74.
WRITE USING 'GOD'S EYE VIEW'

This final point of view is a rather appealing one: in it, the humble writer of a novel, sitting in his or her pyjamas in front of the word-processor, becomes a deity. In the God's eye view the narrator sees all and knows all. It is a further extension of the third person unlimited point of view, with the difference that the narrator can now give information that is not accessible to, or witnessed by, any of the characters. Imagine a novel that begins like this:

> In April, dry winds begin to blow over the mesa flats. They agitate the dust and cause the decaying clapboards of the Wemys farmhouse to bang and tumble against each other.

It might develop like this:

> A car came up the drive in a white cloud. Sally Sherlock, just out of beauty college, wished to dispose of the farm as soon as possible and travel to Europe.

The beginning is not dependent on any character's perceptions. Then a character is introduced, and we are privy to some of her thoughts and motivations. In the God's eye view it is possible to zip in and out like this, distant, close, distant, close, as the story requires.

The God's eye view was the traditional choice of eighteenth and nineteenth century novelists, and is still used today. It gives the narrator a special place, sometimes as a character in their own right: in the God's eye view the narrator can sometimes be found moralizing, speculating on the characters and their possible destinies, even soliciting the reader's opinion.

If you are planning a novel with a detached tone, in which there is a great deal of distance between storyteller and characters, which ranges widely across time and space, or which has a deliberately archaic, ironic feel – then promotion to a supreme being may be for you.

LANGUAGE

75.
ACQUIRE A STYLE

Obviously one can't acquire a style just like that. Style has to be worked for.

'Style' really has three meanings. It may mean:

- The generalized manner of a piece of writing: the way a romantic novel is written, for instance.
- The handling of various technical aspects of language: the use of the passive voice, for example, or the deployment of paragraphs. Depending on who you listen to, there will be preferred ways of handling these technical matters (see the next section).
- The particular and individual 'voice' that emerges from these choices and makes one writer distinctive from others.

It is this third meaning that I wish to focus on here. This third sort of style adds greatly to the pleasure the reader derives from a novel. This was summed up by Blaise Pascal when he said: 'When we see a natural style we are quite surprised and delighted, for we expected to see an author and we find a man.' In other words, if an author has the courage to write 'naturally' – out of his or her own personality – the reader experiences the text as a personal encounter, not as a lecture that could have been given by anyone. In this sense Gertrude Stein has a style, Angela Carter has a style, and Raymond Carver has a style. Read one page from any of them and you know immediately who it is.

The presence of style in this third sense may be a very hard-won thing. Writers, like children learning to talk, often start by imitating others. This is not necessarily a mistake (everyone's got to start somewhere), but good writers reach a point where they realize they must find their own style. And so, screwing their courage to the sticking-place, they begin the journey of exploration into themselves as literary personalities. If that journey is a success, that's when 'instead of an author, we find a man' (or woman).

Style only comes with much practice. It emerges from the lonely hours – thousands of them – sitting at the desk. Style, in the end, is about getting to know yourself as a writer and as a person. As Gore Vidal said: 'Style is knowing who you are, what you want to say, and not giving a damn.' Style is respect for oneself.

76.
WHAT ARE THE RULES OF STYLE?

There is another meaning of style, as discussed in the previous section. It's less to do with the creation of an individual 'voice' and more to do with the technical aspects of writing.

Various commentators have published style guides for writers. Among the best-known are Henry Fowler's *Dictionary of Modern English Usage* and Strunk and White's *Elements of Style*. Newspapers and magazines such as *The Guardian* and *The Economist* produce their own 'house' style guides.

Good style, as promulgated in these kinds of books, is generally distinct from correct grammar and punctuation (see the next section). Style is what you do with language once you have mastered grammar. Style guides therefore include rules such as: never use the passive when the active will do; organize your paragraphs by topic; cut out needless words.

Are these sorts of rules of any value to the novelist?

In my opinion they can be valuable in helping writers to

write clearly, economically and unpretentiously. They can help make your prose less awkward or muddled. However, there is a caveat. Fashions change, and stylistic fashions change with them. Sometimes a 'good' style is lifeless and airless. Style guides are useful to get you thinking about language and the options open to you. However, you should not let them lay down the law about what you must or must not do, especially when you are writing a novel. A novelist thrives on freedom, and that includes stylistic freedom.

77.
UNDERSTAND THE BASICS OF GRAMMAR AND PUNCTUATION

As mentioned above, good style is distinct from correct grammar and punctuation. Style is generally a matter of choice. Correct grammar and punctuation are what you should produce to be acceptable to the reading public (and to agents and editors). Examples of some rules of correct grammar and punctuation are:

- a verb must agree with its subject (you don't tend to write: 'he kick football')
- an uncountable noun such as 'music' or 'rice' takes a singular verb and is not used with the indefinite article (you don't tend to write: 'a nice music are playing')
- you don't use an apostrophe to form a plural (you don't tend to write: 'carrot's thirty pence a pound')

Of course, it's not necessary to use correct grammar in passages of dialogue, since people often speak ungrammatically. Nor, in fact, do you need to use correct grammar or punctuation in narrative prose if you are striving for a particular effect: many of the greatest writers have ridden roughshod over grammar and punctuation. However, they were doing it deliberately, perhaps to create a first person narrator with an unusual 'voice'.

Should writers really get very worried over this sort of thing? Isn't grammar and punctuation something of a straitjacket, a barrier to free expression?

My personal opinion is that the rules must be mastered before they are broken. Grammar and punctuation are there to promote clarity and to help you communicate effectively.

Good grammar and perfect punctuation also serve another function for an aspiring writer. Like it or not, they signal to the professionals who control your destiny (agents, editors, publishers) that you have mastered your craft and deserve to be accorded respect and attention.

A full treatment of the rules of grammar and punctuation is of course outside the scope of this book, but those interested may like to refer to Michael Swan's *Basic English Usage*, or, for a more humorous and informal approach, Lynne Truss' *Eats, Shoots and Leaves*.

A couple of the most misunderstood points of grammar are dealt with briefly in the two following two sections: comma splices and split infinitives.

78.
AVOID THE DREADED COMMA SPLICE

When they read a new manuscript, editors and agents are looking for one thing above all others: an excuse to reject it. This may sound harsh, but it's true, unfortunately. Editors and agents receive so many manuscripts, and have so little time, that they want reasons, quickly, to return them to their authors.

Poor grammar is high on the list of reasons to reject a manuscript. And the comma splice is among the most common of all grammatical mistakes.

A comma splice consists in using a comma to join two grammatically complete clauses. Here are some examples:

- He went home alone, the night had been a failure.
- 'Gak' is getting more popular, three out of four people have tried it.
- I want to raise funds for donkeys, it's really cruel the way they are treated.
- This is his first film, I really recommend it.

You'll notice that each half of the sentence makes sense on its own: it's grammatically complete. A comma is too weak to make that fact clear. The situation can be remedied by replacing the comma with a full stop, a semi-colon, a dash or a conjunction. Thus:

- He went home alone. The night had been a failure.
- 'Gak' is getting more popular; three out of four people have tried it.
- I want to raise funds for donkeys – it's really cruel the way they are treated.
- This is his first film and I really recommend it.

Conjunctions such as 'and', 'so', 'for', 'but', 'yet', 'since', 'because', 'although' and 'or' are strong enough to replace the comma, but conjunctive adverbs such as 'however', 'moreover', 'consequently', 'namely', 'nevertheless' and 'furthermore' are not. 'She hates bacon, however she loves pork' contains a comma splice, but 'She hates bacon, but she loves pork' does not.

Comma splices can be acceptable in dialogue, because people don't always speak in grammatically perfect sentences. It's fine to write, for instance:

Vlad smiled. 'This is my favourite restaurant, the liver is great.'

79.
AVOID THE EQUALLY DREADED SPLIT INFINITIVE

The split infinitive has something in common with the comma splice. It signals to an editor that you may not know quite what you are doing.

An infinitive, in grammar, is a verb with the word 'to' in front of it. 'To work', 'to sleep', to love', 'to hate' and 'to eat' are all infinitives. A split infinitive occurs when something comes between the 'to' and the verb. 'To boldly go where no man has gone before' contains a split infinitive. Splitting your infinitives is considered to be wrong, but there is no good reason why. It's just a convention. And in fact many writers deliberately rebel against the convention. They aim 'to boldly split infinitives that no man had split before', as Douglas Adams put it.

In fact, the situation is even more absurd. When it comes to split infinitives, you will find very few professionals – editors, agents, publishers, writers or teachers – who are prepared to condemn them publicly. That would seem far too stiff and Victorian. But many will nevertheless condemn them privately, because they seem to show that the writer doesn't quite know what they are doing. And while this is so, writers should avoid them.

In summary, keep your 'to' and your verb glued together, and rearrange your sentences if necessary. Don't write:

I plan to completely revise this novel by Christmas.

Write:

I plan to revise this novel completely by Christmas.

80.
TREAT ADJECTIVES AND ADVERBS WITH CAUTION

One final aspect of language is worth looking at in this brief survey for novelists: the treatment of adjectives and adverbs.

A couple of rough-and-ready definitions:

- An adjective is a word that describes a noun.
- An adverb is a word that describes a verb, adjective or other adverb.

Let's take adjectives first. Adjectives, in the hands of a skilled writer, can add a great deal to a piece of writing. I can say 'a lion' or I can go further and say 'a hungry lion'. That adjective, 'hungry', is doing its job: there is a world of difference between a lion and a hungry lion. Dylan Thomas opens *Under Milk Wood* by talking about the 'sloeblack, slow, black, crowblack, fishingboat-bobbing sea', and I think it would probably have been unwise for anyone to have told him: 'Very nice, Dylan, but too many adjectives.'

All right so far. But in the hands of an unskilled writer adjectives may become superfluous. How about 'the furious roar of the aircraft engine'? Most roars are furious, aren't they? Or 'the dead corpse of my uncle'? Even worse: corpses are exclusively dead. The adjectives here merely add excess baggage. They weigh the prose down.

Adverbs, like adjectives, can be a useful tool in a writer's box. For example, an adverb may give a metaphorical dimension to a verb. How about 'The caterpillar ambled donnishly down the stalk'? Or 'He ate with intellectual movements of his fork'? ('with intellectual movements of his fork' is an adverbial phrase). Adverbs may also give a creative counterpoint to the verb or the general context, as in 'She slept furiously in the loft' or 'The clock ticked deafeningly' or '"I hate you," he said brightly.'

But while adverbs can be useful and colourful, they can also inflict damage on a piece of writing. They may, like adjectives, be redundant. 'Scream loudly' would be an example. When is a scream not loud? How about 'whimpered plaintively'? Or 'sauntered casually'? Or 'scribbled hastily'?

The fact that adjectives and adverbs are often described as 'qualifying' gives you an idea of why they should be treated with caution. Anything that qualifies may draw force away from something.

In summary, nouns and verbs are the engines of prose, and they should be allowed to drive it forward without too many restrictions.

OTHER THINGS TO CONSIDER

81.
MANAGE THE FLOW OF TIME

A novel begins at the beginning, meanders through the middle, and concludes with the end. Or does it? As already pointed out, there's more than one way to manage time in a novel. You can start with a beginning that isn't really a beginning, for example. You can skip back and forth through time. Novels often do.

One time-dislocation technique is to hook the reader with an action scene and then go back in time to explain how it came about. Chapter One, for example, might begin with a car-bomb explosion, and Chapter Two explain the backstory of the families caught up in it.

The World According to Garp by John Irving opens with the information that the author's mother was once arrested for stabbing a man in a cinema. There follows several pages of backstory before we find out exactly why she stabbed the man. This is a similar device, which on this occasion is used to generate suspense.

Flashback is probably the most common device used in novels for shifting time-frame. Many novels, especially first-person novels, are told as memoirs, and memoirs lend themselves naturally to a two-stream approach: the events that are happening now as the narrator tells the story, and the events that happened then in the story itself. In *Cakes and Ale* by W Somerset Maugham, the narrator goes back to a number of different times – to his childhood, to his young manhood and to his recent adulthood – while also narrating scenes that happened in the very recent past – the 'yesterday' of the novel. What we get is a sense of multiple plots happening at once, each with their own narrative suspense. Flashbacks are often criticized for deflecting attention from the main plot and thus defusing tension, but, if handled carefully, they can also be suspenseful, since they may withhold information that arrives in the next flashback.

Flashbacks, however, should be proper scenes and not just excuses the provision of information necessary to the plot: sometimes called 'information dumps.' Use action and dialogue in your flashbacks if at all possible. That way they will gain immediacy.

How about if the plot is too frenetic? Try slowing the pace by interposing a scene of reflection between scenes of action. I've always found that it's a good idea to write a novel through at the pace it seems to demand, and then, at the revision stage, read it for narrative pace. If I can see moments that would benefit from a less frenetic scene, I introduce one. That way the novel gains contrast. On the other hand, if the plot is too slow, I blue-pencil the transitional scenes (coach journeys, pointless dialogue, etc.) and cut to the chase.

82.
WRITE IN THE PRESENT TENSE?

Most novels are written in the past tense. They tell a story which is presumed to have happened already. Novels written in the past tense always begin, in a sense, at the end.

However, it's possible to write a novel entirely in the present tense. Here the narrator does not implicitly know how the story ends: they are seemingly discovering the story at the same time as you, the reader. *Room* by Emma Donoghue is one example, a novel in which a young boy is imprisoned with his mother in a single room; the use of the present tense adds to the sense of confinement, since we are never sure that there will ever be a contrasting future state of freedom to look back from. Other examples of present-tense novels are *Lottery* by Patricia Wood and *Wolf Hall* by Hilary Mantel. The style has been around a long time: Dickens and Charlotte Brontë also wrote passages of their novels in the present tense.

The advantages of the present tense are easy to see. There is a gain in immediacy, a certain breathlessness that lends itself very well to certain sorts of narratives, or certain sorts of narrators, particularly unsophisticated or young ones, perhaps with a limited or naïve understanding of the world.

However, one piece of advice: if deciding to opt for a present-tense narrative, consider using it as one tense among many rather than going for an all-out present-tense novel. That way you can benefit from the advantages of past-tense writing too. Present tense can be reserved for the stream-of-consciousness thoughts of a character, or the moments when action needs to be accelerated or played out with hallucinatory vividness. Whole novels written in the present tense may finally lose immediacy, and evoke merely a monotonous incarceration in the present moment.

83.
WRITE A SEX SCENE

Every year since 1993, the *Literary Review* has judged a Bad Sex Award. Its intention is 'to draw attention to the crude, tasteless, often perfunctory use of redundant passages of sexual description in the modern novel, and to discourage it'. Its first winner was Melvyn Bragg.

It seems that some people feel there is too much sex in the modern novel – that it has somehow become mandatory to write sex scenes, regardless of their bearing on the plot. 'Bad sex', according to this view, occurs because authors are writing in an unthinking manner about something essentially irrelevant.

The counter-argument might run as follows: it's important to write about sex in a novel because sex is what most people are thinking about much of the time. As Wallace Shawn put it: 'When someone interested in geology is alone in a room, he or she tends to think a lot about rocks.' And sex is not only a powerful preoccupation for many people but a powerful motivating force, which is important for novelists (see section 33).

Sex also produces conflict (see section 40). We may

desire persons who are nominally attached to other persons, for example. We may espouse the rights of persons to do certain things that others would deny them, and would possibly punish severely (fill in the blanks here with anything from Auto-eroticism to Zoophilia).

So if you lean towards this latter side of the debate, how do you approach sex in your writing? One traditional approach has been by using humour. But humour may be a defense mechanism. It's more difficult to write seriously about sex.

Another avenue would be to would be to write obliquely rather than directly. Not necessarily out of prudishness, but for a higher sexual voltage. It's rather like the difference between the erotic and the pornographic: 'The erotic is using a feather while the pornographic is using the whole chicken.' The former may be sexier than the latter. A scene where sex doesn't happen can be 3000% sexier than one in which it does.

Sex should also be integrated into the lives of the characters and the plot. As Anaïs Nin said: 'Without feelings, inventions, moods, no surprises in bed. Sex must be mixed with tears, laughter, words, promises, scenes, jealousy, envy, all the spices of fear, foreign travel, new faces, novels, stories, dreams, fantasies, music, dancing, opium, wine.'

The greatest commandment is surely this: don't let anyone dictate to you what is or is not acceptable, not even the *Literary Review*.

84.
CONTROL YOUR NOVEL'S EMOTIONAL CONTENT

Think about the last novel you enjoyed. What effect did it have on you? It almost certainly moved you in some way. When you put it down after reading the last page, you were probably still vibrating from the way it elicited emotions of horror, or pity, or pathos, or amazement, or sadness, or wonder.

It might be said that this is the novelist's job: to bring about these emotions in the breasts of their readers. The novelist seeks not to persuade readers, through argument, to adopt a particular view of life, but to grab them and make them feel. The short-story writer Guy de Maupassant said: 'The public is composed of numerous groups who cry to us: "Console me; amuse me; make me sad; make me sympathetic; make me dream; make me laugh; make me shudder; make me weep; make me think.""

Writing a novel then may be conceived of as a campaign to make readers feel. How to do it?

Firstly you can appeal to basic human fascinations such as sex and death. Play on these drives and you will very quickly produce a strong emotional effect. Romance and crime writers do this all the time, though the effect may, in the end, be merely the thrill of melodrama.

Secondly you can appeal to the senses (see section 87). What is intensely described through taste, touch, sight, hearing or smell can also elicit strong emotion. Further, sensory details may have a psychic element. A disgusting smell may shade very readily into moral disgust, for example. Try to show your characters responding emotionally to what they sense.

Thirdly you can use imagery (see section 89), which, as discussed, bypasses, to an extent, the rational mind.

Fourthly you can elicit emotion with suspense (see section 38). Suspense is, at root, the emotion of excited curiosity.

I believe though that the greatest emotional writing comes from fully-imagined characterization. If your characters are real and believable, then their emotional lives will be real and believable too. Now you can bring in those above-mentioned drives of sex and death and they will have their maximum impact. Give your characters potent drives and daunting obstacles to their fulfilment. Prepare the ground carefully enough and your readers will be taken, body and soul, into a new world of feeling.

85.
GIVE YOUR NOVEL A SENSE OF PLACE

How do you describe a novel? 'It's a coming-of-age story set in Moldova'. 'It's set in a holiday camp in Great Yarmouth in the 1950s.' The place – the setting – is often an important part of the way a novel exists in the mind of its readers.

'Place' and 'setting' are slightly different terms. 'Place' suggests a town, a country, a locality. 'Setting' can be smaller, more intimate – a café, the inside of a coach, a room – but also include the wider world: a café within a town, a room within a tower block.

Does an evocation of place do anything more than provide colour in a novel? Indeed it does. Place can have a key relationship to plot. The country house murder plot is impossible without the country house setting, because the house is an island, cut off by the tide: no one can arrive or depart without notice. Place can also have a key relationship to characters. In a city of rank alleyways, certain characters breed. But perhaps not quite the ones you expect. A slum may engender order and harmony as opposed to chaos and crime. A crowded bar, from the outside like a party, is actually full of knots of people who don't know one another.

Place can be a character, almost, in its own right. The Polish shtetl is a character in the short stories of Isaac Bashevis Singer. The provincial backwater is a character in Chekhov. Blandings Castle or the Drones Club are characters in Wodehouse.

In describing a place likely to be unfamiliar to your readers, it's the texture of the everyday that is important. What are the plug sockets like? How do men and women touch each other in public? What's on the stamps? In describing a place that is likely to be familiar to your readers, on the other hand, you really do have your work cut out. Readers need to be challenged with some new perception. You can do this most effectively by focussing on detail, particularly detail with a sensory element. Something ordinary, but observed in an extraordinary way; something that will make us interested even though we've been to the place – or a place seemingly like it – a thousand times.

A few strokes are generally preferable to an exhaustive description. If your characters are in a bar, don't describe the whole bar, with all its furniture, people, mirrors, bottles, etc. Give one detail that does the job of ten. A cobweb on the underside of the bar; the sticky sound your sole makes as you detach it from the foot-rail.

86.
GIVE YOUR NOVEL A SENSE OF SPACE

In *Aspects of the Novel*, EM Forster distinguishes between a sense of place (which many novelists have, or try to cultivate) and a sense of space (which fewer novelists have, or try to cultivate). He cites Tolstoy as an example:

> [*War and Peace*] has extended over space as well as over time, and the sense of space until it terrifies us is exhilarating, and leaves behind it an effect like music. After one has read *War and Peace* for a bit, great chords begin to sound [...] They come from the immense area of Russia, over which episodes and characters have been scattered, from the sum-total of bridges and frozen rivers, forests, roads, gardens, fields, which accumulate grandeur and sonority after we have passed them.

Tolstoy allows his eye to roll over a vast area, geographically; one couldn't achieve the same effect of space by having a vast roll-call of characters in a small village.

Modern novelists with a sense of space are usually those writing in the historical, sci-fi or fantasy genres: one might mention Tolkien's *Lord of the Rings* trilogy, Paul Scott's *Raj Quartet* or *The English Patient* by Michael Ondaatje. Length of novel (or series of novels) seems to be related to the sense of space, since it's only in a long novel or series of novels that there is room for the sub-plots and para-plots that take place in many different, but interrelated locations over a wide area. It's difficult to conceive of a novella with a sense of space, though it may have a fully-developed sense of place.

87.
EMPHASIZE SENSE DATA

Sight, smell, touch, taste and hearing. There may be a sixth, but no one can agree what it is. For now, we're stuck with five.

But these five are the basis of art. Art is about feeling: feeling in the fingers, in the bone, in the bone marrow. Of course, art is also about ideas – but it can't stay in that rarefied zone for long. When art leaves the realm of the mind and enters the world of the senses, it comes alive; it is suddenly accessible to everyone. If you write using sense data, you immediately touch your readers.

Look at that arch-rationalist George Orwell's essay 'Down the Mine', for example.

> There is the heat – it varies, but in some mines it is suffocating – and the coal dust that stuffs up your throat and your nostrils and collects along your eyelids, and the unending rattle of the conveyor-belt, which in that confined space is rather like the rattle of a machine-gun. But the fillers look and work as though they were made of iron. They really

do look like iron – hammered iron statues...The first time I was watching the 'fillers' at work I put my hand upon some dreadful slimy thing among the coal dust. It was a chewed quid of tobacco.

Here, in an ostensibly polemical piece, Orwell makes intense appeals to the senses of sight, hearing, touch, and, implicitly, taste and smell (the coal dust in the throat and nostrils).

If you make appeals to the senses your readers may feel any of several things:

- They may discover an experience for the first time.
- They may remember something they've forgotten.
- They may experience the thrill of having a common experience put into words for the first time ('what oft was thought but ne'er so well expressed').
- They may feel a strong sense of the writer behind the words; because in describing an object intensely and sensually, the writer reveals himself or herself.

You stand more of a chance of moving your audience if you describe a small particular thing with reference to its individual sensual reality than a large, impersonal, abstract idea.

88.
THINK ABOUT SYMBOLS

A symbol is a concrete thing that stands in for (usually) an abstract thing. In everyday life, a wedding ring symbolizes marriage, a bald eagle symbolizes America, a cross symbolizes Christianity and a kitemark symbolizes safety.

In literature, symbols are used to add depth and power to writing, and to act as a sort of shorthand for ideas. In *Lord of the Flies* by William Golding, the conch shell symbolizes order and civilization, and when, towards the end of the book, the conch is shattered, we know that the forces of misrule have finally gained the ascendant: the shattering of the conch is a terrifying moment because Golding has been careful to invest the conch with symbolic freight.

If you choose to adopt symbols in your writing, you should try to avoid the obvious. A crow may represent death, but if you have a crow come and sit on your character's shoulder as a prediction of their imminent demise, the moment will probably seem farcical.

If you wish to invent a symbol, think first about the abstract ideas that already exist within your novel. For example, you may already have touched on greed, ambition, love, failure, bereavement, the burden of past deeds, the importance of familial bonds, manhood, womanhood, concern for the environment or the power of art. The symbol you use to stand for any of these ideas may be drawn from any area of life, but will almost always be a concrete thing. It may be a natural object such as a river, a fire, a storm or the moon; an artefact such as a clock, a ring, a key or a mirror; an animal such as a dog, a lion, a donkey or a cat; or, less concrete but still tied to the physical world, an action such as burning a photograph or climbing a tower. The choices are legion. For example, if your novel is about a council that wishes to build a bypass and is opposed by local campaigners, the leader of the council can be shown obsessively trimming the topiary hedge in his front garden. The topiary symbolizes his desire to control – and by extension society's desire to control – the natural world.

Symbols do not have fixed meanings. You decide what they mean. Conventionally the colour red symbolizes passion, but you may wish it to symbolize hope. If you wish to make this connection, introduce the colour red at hopeful moments, or in conjunction with hopeful signs. It is the frequent extended correspondence between the signifier and the signified that makes symbolism what it is. There is nothing inherent in a conch that symbolizes civilisation, after all; Golding had to work hard to integrate the conch into the story to establish its importance.

89.
USE IMAGERY

Imagery is a general term to describe literary effects such as metaphor, simile, personification, metonymy, synecdoche, and so on, most of which were codified thousands of years ago by Greeks. Imagery really comes into its own in poetry, but may also be found in prose writing. Two classes of image are especially important for novelists: metaphor and simile.

Metaphor is an explicit statement of identity between one thing and another. If I say 'he's a pig' or 'the moon was a gold coin in the sky' I am using metaphor. Note that I am not saying 'he is like a pig' or 'the moon was like a gold coin in the sky': I am making a more powerful and direct claim of identity between the two. It is such a powerful claim, in fact, that it forces the reader to suspend rationality for a moment, allowing emotion to flood in to fill the gap. If I say 'the moon was snared in the branches of the tree', the branches of the tree seem malevolently to grasp the moon, in defiance of our rational understanding of trees, moons or perspective.

But this may be too violent an effect for a novel.

Simile is more useful in prose. A simile uses the words 'like' or 'as' to suggest a comparison between two things.

If I say 'her lips were as red as blood' or 'he shut the door like a priest closing a Bible' then I am using simile. Both of these would sit easily in a novel. But many of the hoariest clichés in the English language are similes. I've already given one: 'as red as blood'. Others are: as blind as a bat, as ugly as sin, like a headless chicken, as drunk as a lord, like a bat out of hell, as mad as a hatter...the list could be extended to the end of this page and beyond. For that reason, when a writer rings the changes on these tired glad-rags of language (to mix metaphors for a moment) he or she can produce some startling effects. How about – as blind as a piecrust, as ugly as Ipswich, like a headless estate agent, as drunk as a newsreader, like a bat out of a biscuit tin, as mad as a train (a loco?). These rely on surprise for their effect (because we are expecting something else), but good similes will often be startling, sometimes humorously so, perhaps even surreally so. To say of a small person that 'he looked like a troll whose bridge had collapsed' is to give an immediately arresting picture which is disquietingly specific.

Novelists use similes because they demonstrate a certain poetic virtuosity. Even so they should be used sparingly. A page that has been totally stuffed with similes will take the reader into a realm of linguistic fireworks where the novel itself has temporarily been forgotten. If that's the sort of novel you're writing, fair enough. If not, be careful.

90.
CHOOSE A GOOD TITLE

A title, in the simplest understanding of its function, is there to advertise the contents of a book. That's why *Brideshead Revisited* is called *Brideshead Revisited* – because it's about revisiting Brideshead. *How to Cook in a Small Flat* will very probably be about how to prepare joyless meals on a single hotplate while trying to stave off pneumonia, and if it's not, the reader will justifiably feel cheated.

There's another obvious qualification a title should have: brevity. It should fit on the book, particularly on the spine. It's rather interesting that early novels didn't have covers as they exist today. The title information was given inside, on the title page. This meant that titles were mini-summaries of what lay inside the book. What we refer to today as *Robinson Crusoe* was originally called *The Life and Strange Surprizing Adventures of Robinson Crusoe of York, Mariner: Who Lived Eight and Twenty Years, All Alone in an Un-inhabited Island on the Coast of America, near the Mouth of the Great River of Oroonoque.*

A third qualification is that a title should be enticing. It should make you want to pick up the book. At the same time it should not be an obvious gimmick, since that tends to put people off. A difficult balancing act to achieve.

So just to recap, three basic qualifications for a title – not the only ones, but important ones in our present literary epoch – are that it should be brief, descriptive and enticing. Many successful titles manage all three: *The Lion, the Witch and the Wardrobe*, *Waiting for Godot*, *The World According to Garp*, *My Family and Other Animals*, *Lady Chatterley's Lover* and *Pride and Prejudice*. These are all well-engineered titles.

But hold on – if these books had been called something else, wouldn't they have been just as successful? Unfortunately it's impossible to tell without re-running literary history. Actually, literary history shows us that finding a title is often a rather hit-and-miss affair. Titles we think of as firmly part of the western canon – such as *Catch-22* or *Murder in the Cathedral* – would, but for a fluke, have been very different. Anyone for *Catch-18* or *Fear in the Way*?

Perhaps the last word should go to Maxwell Perkins, the legendary editor of Hemingway and Fitzgerald:

> The title is extremely important, and since there is no logical process by which one may be discovered, it often presents great difficulties... We have often had great struggles over a title, and thought it might be a bad one. Then the title has succeeded supremely, and it seemed the only title that was conceivable for it.

REVISING
YOUR WORK

91.
EDIT, EDIT, EDIT

Vladimir Nabokov said: 'I have rewritten – often several times – every word I have ever published. My pencils outlast their erasers.'

Most novels are written not once but again and again. Most writers revise, and revise, and revise, seeking to make their work as good as it can possibly be.

This sounds like hard work, but revising is actually more fun than it sounds. The revision stage is when you look at your work, congratulate yourself on what you've achieved, and then build on it. Personally, I enjoy revising. After all the labour of trying to conjure up characters and situations from thin air, revising is like a holiday.

A clarification is needed here, though. There are really two kinds of revision. The first involves the small edits, word changes, paragraph repositionings and adjective deletions that are done when wiser counsel prevails. You can do this as you go along: in fact, I find it helpful to edit the previous day's work before starting on any new writing, since it helps me immerse myself in the world of my story and limbers up my writing muscles.

The second kind, however, involves major structural changes: alterations of point of view, the insertion or deletion of major characters, the change of locations. It involves addressing the novel as a whole, either as a first draft or as a serious chunk of writing. If you can leave a delay before going back to do major revision, it will almost certainly benefit you. Put your novel on a shelf for a month or two, and then return to it with a fresh eye. You will see much more clearly where it could be improved, and you will also have acquired a necessary degree of ruthlessness; distance from your everyday struggles will give you the courage to cut and change with broad strokes.

Revision is often about cutting (see the next section for the main things to cut), but it is also about expansion. When you are really imaginatively caught up in telling a story, you might write rapidly, telling it in 'skeleton' form as you rush from one plot development to the next. Only later do you go back and add material, filling in what needs explaining, solidifying characterization and adding descriptions.

Be careful here, though: something you add can dislocate other parts of the book. A character may have cropped hair at the beginning of the book and a few pages later it may be at waist level. Also look for consistency in dates, seasons and weather. Is someone wearing a T-shirt in Edinburgh in January?

92.
CUT, CUT, CUT

As mentioned in the previous section, much of your revision will involve cutting.

In a way, this is inevitable. Writing is about exploring and risk-taking; some explorations will reach dead ends, and some risks won't pay off. These failed experiments must be pruned. It can be very painful to cut what you have spent a lot of time over, but you must think of it in terms of the good of the finished product, and be brutal: cut out whole pages or chapters if they seem to intrude or break up the flow. A novel is not like an exam in which you must 'show your workings'.

Here are some things to look for when cutting:

• Exposition. This is the dreaded 'information dump' in which you regale your reader with your research: historical information, technical details of a subject, the family pedigrees of your characters. These are 'the parts that readers tend to skip'.
• Pointless dialogue. Cut conversations that don't lead anywhere, don't advance characterization or develop the plot, or which have no tension.

- Overblown descriptions. Remember Robert Louis Stevenson's remark about scenery, that we hear too much of it in novels. Similarly with opulent descriptions of buildings or interiors. Single telling details can be much more effective.
- Characters who don't seem to be contributing much or are too much like other characters. Characters should, if possible, have a job to do. If one character loses a key, at least consider the possibility that the person who finds it in the street could be someone who later crops up and has a role in the plot, and not someone insignificant who we never hear from again.
- Anything deliberately obscure. Readers will not generally appreciate arcane references designed to be comprehensible to .01% of the reading public, or baffling foreign words intended to impart exoticism.
- 'Over-writing' – see the next section on 'murdering your darlings'.

Finally, don't throw away the material you cut. Something that is cut from one place may belong in another. Put your cuttings in a scrap file. Even if you never use this material, it could still be useful. Re-reading your scrap file may serve to remind you of something about your character or plot that you could do differently.

93.
MURDER YOUR DARLINGS

Sir Arthur Quiller-Couch in his book *On the Art of Writing* (1916) talked about a Persian lover who hired a professional letter-writer to convey his passion. The letter-writer produced a missive dripping with fulsome vocabulary and courtly turns of phrase. Sir Arthur went on:

> Well, in this extraneous, professional, purchased ornamentation, you have something which Style is not: and if you here require a practical rule of me, I will present you with this: 'Whenever you feel an impulse to perpetrate a piece of exceptionally fine writing, obey it – whole-heartedly – and delete it before sending your manuscript to press. Murder your darlings.'

In other words, if something you've written seems particularly excellent, it may be a prime candidate for cutting.

That doesn't mean that everything that satisfies you is bad. But you should subject these 'darlings', these fine turns of phrase, to very close scrutiny. A startling image, for example, in which one thing is compared bizarrely to another, may seem like a flash of genius at the time, but cooler consideration will reveal that it disrupts the flow of the story, especially if it follows hard on the heels of another bizarre image, or just doesn't fit with the general tone of the book. Intrusions of an authorial voice saying something amusing, or reflecting on how the book is going, should also usually be considered very carefully. And purple passages in which locations are established may be a little yawn-inducing.

In short, look for the things you are most pleased with, and ask yourself why they seem to stand out so much. It may be because they don't belong there.

94.
HANDLE AND USE FEEDBACK

Feedback can be an important part of the revision process. It's important to get it at the right time, though. If feedback arrives when you're composing rather than revising, it may be counterproductive. It may warp the growth of a book, sending it off in a direction you didn't intend, or stunting and stopping it altogether. Negative feedback at the wrong time, when you are feeling vulnerable, can damage your confidence. So make sure, before you ask advice on changing things, that you really are ready to change things.

How do you ask for feedback? Well, if you are a member of a writers' group, that will pose no problem (see section 11). Friends and family members can offer useful insights too. They may not be skilled critics, but most people in the general public are not skilled critics either, and they are the ones who will be buying your book.

When soliciting feedback, it's a good idea to ask for feedback on a certain thing. For example, you can ask: how well did you think the point of view works in this piece?

Did the dialogue convince you? Do you understand what motivates the main character? This kind of question focusses the reader, encouraging them to say specific things rather than offering blanket praise or condemnation ('I loved it' or 'It didn't really work for me'). You can even ask general questions designed to enable you, the author, to see the book afresh: 'Can you describe this book?' 'What, if anything, is this book about?'

How do you respond to feedback? In the first instance, don't. Don't argue with your respondent. Instead, listen, draw them out and encourage them. Thank them and take the feedback away. You have gone to some lengths to obtain it, so now consider carefully what it can offer.

Feedback is likely to be a mixed bag. Most readers won't say outright that your novel is all wrong; neither will they say that it's all great and there are no faults. They may offer a 'praise sandwich' (a criticism flanked by two mollifying slices of praise). If they do this, peel open the sandwich and look inside. The filling represents their true opinion. Examine it as a critic would. Is their argument backed up by the facts? What examples have they drawn on? Are they supported by other examples? Did they understand what the novel was trying to achieve, and if not, does the fault lie with you?

Feedback is an important tool in the process of sifting and weighing your work, but not the only one, or necessarily the most important. In the final analysis, you must be the judge of your own work – at any rate, till your editor gets his hands on it.

WHAT TO DO WITH YOUR NOVEL

95.
WRITE A NOVEL SYNOPSIS

A novel synopsis is similar to a plot summary, in that it gives a précis of all the events that happen in the novel. Unlike a plot summary, however (which is a private document written to manage the plot during the process of composition: see section 47), a novel synopsis is there to help you sell your book.

Agents and publishers don't always have the time to read whole novels. They will prefer in many cases to be sent a couple of sample chapters plus a synopsis. If they like what they read, they might then ask to be sent the whole novel.

Synopses are also useful for agents and publishers to give to others: for example jacket designers, blurb writers and sales reps, who might not wish to spend their time reading the whole novel but will still need to know what it's about.

A synopsis should contain all the events in the novel, including the ending (spoil away to your heart's content). It should do justice to the plot without being too long. For a complex novel, the synopsis might be as much as 3,000 words (10 double-spaced pages). For something simpler, perhaps only 1,000 words (3 pages). You can divide the synopsis into chapters for ease of reference, or tell the story straight through, in lots of short paragraphs. Set out the book as it happens, using the present tense ('Chapter Four: Ricky goes to Marlene's and tells her he loves her. Marlene is offended.') Use your strong opening (see section 51) as a way of getting the agent or publisher interested: remember, this synopsis is the first thing they will read. So include your initial dilemma, death, journey, challenge or discovery, and say why it has an impact on your character.

> Jenny Turner, 58, a marketing manager due at
> an important conference, wakes up in a shipping
> container and can't remember how she got there.
> She bangs on the walls but no one can hear her.
> In desperation she begins to explore her new
> environment.

Then continue through your novel with all the salient details of character and plot. Don't include dialogue or anything inessential.

It's important to stress here that a synopsis is not a substitute for a finished novel. A first-time author will very rarely sell a novel on the basis of a synopsis alone. They will still need the completed novel to back it up. A successful and established novelist may be able to sell a novel on the basis of sample chapters and a synopsis, but such beings are among the elite few who can guarantee an audience of thousands before they put pen to paper.

96.
PRESENT AND SUBMIT YOUR MANUSCRIPT

After you have written your novel and your novel synopsis, you need someone to send it to.

Whether you first approach an agent (see the next section) or go direct to a publisher (see section 98), the method is basically the same. First, write a covering letter or email. This should be brief and businesslike, setting out your previous publishing experience, if any, and giving a one-sentence plot outline of the novel. Don't attempt humour in the covering letter. Pretend you're applying for a job.

Along with the covering letter, send between one and three sample chapters, plus your synopsis. Most submissions these days will be via email, but if you are sending your manuscript by post, send an SAE big enough to contain these on their return journey, with the correct postage.

The documents you send should be double spaced, with adequate margins, and, if printed out, on one side of the paper only. If submitting by email, the synopsis and sample chapters should be separate documents.

If all goes well, and the agent or publisher likes what they read, they will ask for more. You can then post or email the complete manuscript. Keep a copy, naturally. Put your name and email address on the first and last pages of the typescript or e-document, so that if it gets mislaid people will still be able to find you.

Bear in mind a sardonic description by Oliver Herford: 'Manuscript: something submitted in haste and returned at leisure.' You have control only over the first part, so make sure your submission is as unhasty as possible.

97.
FIND A LITERARY AGENT

Agents are held in roughly the same repute as the tax authorities. They take 15% of everything you get, yet they leave you to write the books on your own. It's all very unfair.

But for that fee of 15% (sometimes a little more, sometimes a little less) a literary agent will do a great deal. Firstly, they'll make sure your work is seen by the appropriate publisher. Different publishers publish different things, and it is an agent's job to know what will fit a publisher's list and what won't. Secondly, they'll draw up the best contract for you, and not just in terms of money: an agent will also handle subsidiary rights such as film, television, e-book and serial rights, and keep an eye on foreign markets and potential translations. Thirdly, agents can help to manage all the additional activities that come with being an author, such as speaking engagements, journalism and interviews. And lastly a good agent will offer criticism of your work and be available to talk (and answer your emails).

So how to find one? A personal recommendation from

a fellow-writer is useful, but the standard sources – *The Writers' and Artists' Yearbook* or *The Writer's Handbook* – are also good. Before you make the approach, it's wise to find out whether the agency handles your sort of book. It's no use sending a sci-fi epic to an agent who exclusively represents books on animal husbandry.

Once you've got a list of appropriate agents, send an exploratory letter or email with a synopsis of your project and between two and four sample chapters. If the agent likes what they read, they may invite you to become a client. You will then be expected to sign an agreement setting out matters such as commission fees, territories covered, chargeable expenses (such as buying copies of your book from the publisher for publicity purposes) and the duration of the relationship.

One word of caution: don't pay an agent to read your work. Some disreputable agents survive on reading fees alone, and never place any author with a publisher.

What do agents want in return? They are chiefly looking for a client who can make them money in the long term. Most agents are not in the business of finding one-hit wonders (though if a book is juicy enough, they won't say no). They want writers with careers they can nurture and develop: writers who have the potential to produce a catalogue of work that will provide income over many years.

It is possible to get published without an agent, and many authors successfully represent themselves. But an agent makes publication much more probable. That increased probability alone is worth 15%.

98.
WORK WITH A PUBLISHER

After you or your agent has submitted the manuscript, you must settle back and wait. It can be a long wait. Manuscripts can languish for months in publishers' offices. The average publisher will receive many hundreds, perhaps many thousands of manuscripts a year, and email has greatly increased the volume of submissions.

Publishers employ members of staff to look through this inundation for sparks of luminescence. All manuscripts – unless they are patently unsuitable (fiction for a non-fiction publisher, for example) – will receive at least some level of attention. The role of a publisher is not chiefly to frustrate authors and deny them immortality. Publishers actually want to find good novels.

If your novel is one of them, and the publisher has the wit to recognize it, you may receive a phone call. Amid the congratulations, the publisher may (and probably will) express some reservations. Sometimes the reservations will be major. A substantial re-write may be asked for. You should consider your response carefully. Refusal to co-operate at this stage can still bring about the termination of the agreement.

After any re-write has been completed to everyone's satisfaction, an advance is offered and a contract drawn up (see the next section).

This is not the end. Now editing begins. This process may vary wildly from publisher to publisher. It is possible for a book to go all the way through the editing process without an apostrophe being changed; in other cases, almost every sentence will receive some sort of tweak. Publishers may assign both an in-house and an out-of-house editor to do this work, with the result that authors may have to cope with more than one set of suggestions. (Nowadays editing is usually done on an electronic document where the various editing contributions can be tracked.) This can be a distressing process for the author, but don't dig your heels in if you can help it: these people are genuinely trying to improve your book.

Finally the manuscript will go to proofs. The proof may come in the form of an electronic document such as a pdf, or may be accorded the dignity of a bound proof volume (these latter are useful for reviews and sales reps). A jacket will be designed (over which the author usually has little say) and the title finalized. Finally the day arrives on which the novel is published.

And that's it. It's odd, really. What was once a bundle of worries over plot, conflict, dialogue, structure, symbolism and theme is now a physical object in bookshops.

99.
MANAGE YOUR CONTRACT

Contracts contain information vital to your book's success and your financial health, and should be scrutinized carefully, preferably with some professional help (a literary agent or a member of the contracts vetting team at the Society of Authors). Some of the most important areas are as follows.

Firstly, the advance. This is money that is payable in a lump sum, either on signature of the contract or at some specified point or points afterwards (e.g. on delivery of the work or a year after signature). A typical advance for a first-time author is around £1,000. This sum is set against royalties, so you won't earn any royalties until you 'earn out' the advance. If you never earn enough royalties, the advance is usually non-returnable.

Secondly, the royalties themselves. These vary according to several factors, such as whether the sales are in hardback or paperback editions, or in the 'home' or 'export' market. Royalties tend to increase per book as more copies are sold. Notification of royalties arrives in the form of a royalty statement a year or so after publication.

Thirdly, subsidiary rights. The contract will specify whether the publishers have the right to license publication in various other formats, such as large print editions, book club editions, Braille editions, talking book editions, and so on; further, whether they can sell the book at a later date to another publisher. The subsidiary rights will sometimes keep your novel alive long after the book itself has disappeared from the bookshops. If your book is ever translated or made into a film, the contract will also specify the rights of the various parties and the revenues involved.

Fourthly, delivery and publication. The contract will set out two important dates: the delivery date, by which the author must undertake to get the typescript (or an electronic version of it) to the publisher, and the publication date, by which time the publisher must have published the book.

Fifthly, the territory. For publishing purposes, the world is carved up into territories, and the contract will stipulate in which of these the publisher is allowed to publish your book.

Finally, and of great importance to authors, the jacket. The contract will stipulate whether you have the right of consultation on the book's jacket design. If you do, that's great. But remember, it's only a right of consultation. The publisher is free, after consultation, to ignore you completely!

100.
WORK WITH A NOT-QUITE-PUBLISHER

Not all books are published by publishers. Many famous authors have published their own books. Walt Whitman and Samuel Richardson are two that spring to mind: Walt Whitman even reviewed his own book, Leaves of Grass, describing it as 'this wild, free, reckless voice of the fields'. If you pay to have your own novel printed, you are at least in good company.

The drawback is that if you print your novel yourself you will have to sell it yourself. Publishers don't just print books: they oversee their publicity, promotion, warehousing, distribution and sale. And once you run out of local bookshops to sell your novel to, or run out of relatives, you may find you are building furniture out of the unsold copies.

Paying to have your own book printed is one thing. Approaching a vanity publisher is another. Vanity publishers masquerade as real publishers, with all the paraphernalia of contracts, royalties, subsidiary rights and so on. They tend to place advertisements in newspapers with headlines such as 'Authors wanted' or 'Have you written a novel?' These are a dead giveaway: legitimate publishers do not need to advertise for manuscripts.

When you send your novel to a vanity publisher they will assure you of its brilliance, then ask you for a sum to go towards production costs (which a real publisher will never do). This sum will not just cover costs, but will ensure a profit for the vanity publisher, who will take little or no care over your book. It will never be reviewed or distributed to bookshops. The whole process will inevitably be more expensive than simply printing a few copies yourself.

An alternative is to publish electronically. This strategy has numerous advantages. The first is that it's cheap; in fact it's free to create an e-text that can be sold on Amazon (see Amazon's Digital Text Platform site for details), though you will have to pay a large chunk of the cover-price as a commission. The second advantage is that there are numerous opportunities for self-promotion that don't exist in the hard-copy world: you can give away tantalizing sample chapters for free, for example. The third is that you may find it easier to glean feedback from readers, and there are many supportive online communities (though these can be somewhat self-regarding).

Before you upload, make sure you have revised and edited as you would do with any hard-copy novel. Get a friend to read your book for spelling and punctuation. The drawback of self-publishing is that you will never have an editor who is paid to make your work look as good as possible.

101.
PROMOTE YOUR BOOK

The publishing process doesn't end when the book is published. An author may be expected to do quite a bit of work promoting his or her own book.

The main arenas for authors are: radio, television, literary festivals, journalism and public speaking.

As far as radio is concerned, there are the national stations, of course, but also a very large number of local stations looking for something interesting to fill up airtime. People who listen to the radio read a lot. Requests for interviews may come via agents or publishers: you can also try to generate interest by sending a copy of your book to the radio station's programming department.

If you are invited for a radio interview, try to think of all the questions that could possibly be asked, then write down your answers and practise giving them. The great thing about radio is that you can take your notes into the studio and no one at home knows! As you do more interviews you'll get more adept at speaking extempore.

Television can be more frightening, but unlike much radio, it's not always live, which reduces the tension. It will help if you remember that most people at home are semi-comatose. Also: if you stumble or mess up they'll just think you're eccentric. You're an author, after all!

Literary festivals are everywhere nowadays: there must be one a week somewhere in the UK. If you are fortunate enough to be asked to attend one, jump at it. It's a great way to meet the people who are actually reading your books – which is something radio and TV can't offer. Journalism for authors takes several forms. Authors may be invited to contribute book reviews or opinion pieces, and in some cases may sell serial rights to their book (giving the right to publish excerpts). This can easily double an author's income from a book.

Speaking in public can be rewarding and remunerative. There are over 100 agencies in the UK alone that find speakers for events. They're looking, not necessarily for 'experts', but for authors who have written books. If you've published one, speaking could form a major part of your income.

Some authors enjoy promoting their work, but others find it irksome and would much rather be getting on with writing the next book. In fact, the degree of immersion writers have in their *current* project often makes any past project seem slightly irrelevant. Michael Holroyd said: 'There's something terrible about it really, because you finish a book and it's not published for another year or so... and when people say "What's your book about?" you think "Well, what is my book about?"'

THE ONE HUNDRED AND

THE ONE HUNDRED AND SECOND WAY

102.
THE ONE HUNDRED AND SECOND WAY

There is a thing out there in the literary wilds. It is lawless, ungovernable, savage – perhaps even a little perverted. Nothing that has been said in this book applies to it.

Its name is the anti-novel.

Tristram Shandy is an anti-novel. *To the Lighthouse* is an anti-novel. *Slaughterhouse-Five* is an anti-novel. *Ulysses* is an anti-novel. These novels – among the greatest ever written – delight in taking the rules and dancing all over them.

An anti-novel may contain passages of undigested exposition (see section 58). It may have a long and obscure title that barely fits on the cover (section 90). It may have little or no plot (section 37 onwards). It may deliberately deflate its own suspense (section 38). It may be written from a confusing mixture of viewpoints, so that the reader is never quite sure who is speaking (section 69). It may be deliberately poorly punctuated, comma splices may abound (section 78).

But one thing may be asserted of all these anti-

strategies: they are only possible after the conventions of the novel have been understood. If the conventions are not understood, then what you end up with is not an anti-novel, but a bad novel.

So go ahead and flout the conventions. Ignore everything in this book and do it your own way. But give the conventions a fair hearing first.

That's the only way you are going to write *Ulysses*.

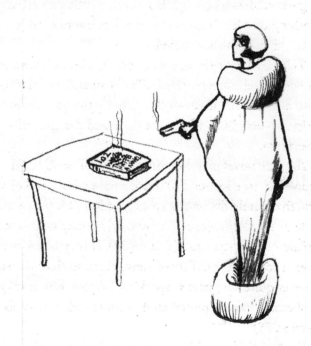

SUGGESTIONS FOR FURTHER READING

Bell, James Scott: *Plot & Structure* (Writers Digest, 2004)

Bernays, Anne, and Painter, Pamela: *What If? Writing Exercise for Fiction Writers* (Collins, 1990)

Brande, Dorothea: *Becoming a Writer* (Harcourt, Brace, 1934)

Card, Orson Scott: *Characters and Viewpoint* (Robinson, 1990)

Doughty, Louise: *A Novel in a Year* (Pocket Books, 2007)

Fairfax, John, and Moat, John: *The Way to Write* (Elm Tree, 1981)

Forster, EM: *Aspects of the Novel* (Edward Arnold, 1927)

Kress, Nancy: *Beginnings, Middles and Ends* (Writer's Digest, 1993)

Kissick, Gary: *Please Set Me Free So I Can Destroy the Earth* (FeedARead)

Leder, Meg, ed.: *The Complete Handbook of Novel Writing* (Writer's Digest, 2002)

Legat, Michael: *An Author's Guide to Publishing* (Robert Hale, 1982)

Legat, Michael: *Plotting the Novel* (Robert Hale, 1992)

Legat, Michael: *Writing for Pleasure and Profit* (Robert Hale, 1986)

Lodge, David: *The Art of Fiction* (Penguin, 1992)

Pullinger, Kate: *How to Write Fiction* (Guardian news and Media, 2008)

Swan, Michael: *Basic English Usage* (OUP, 1984)

Truss, Lynne: *Eats, Shoots and Leaves* (Profile, 2003)

Uzzell, Thomas: *Narrative Technique* (Harcourt, Brace, 1923)

Watts, Nigel: *Writing a Novel* (Teach Yourself Books, 1996)

Winokur, Jon: *Writers on Writing* (Headline, 1986)

General Reference:

The Writers' and Artists' Yearbook (A&C Black, published annually)

The Writer's Handbook (Macmillan, published annually)

A STORY OF LOVE, NUCLEAR TERROR AND THE 1980S ...

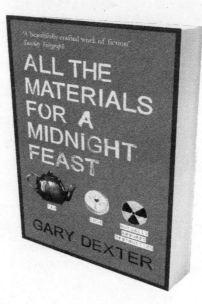

Born at the very height of the Cuban Missile Crisis, Nicholas has lived his life in terror of atomic meltdown. Now, on the eve of his 48th birthday, he is on an overnight coach ride to join an anti-nuclear rally at Faslane in Scotland.

His fellow travellers remind him of his younger self at Hull University in the 1980s. As the coach rolls through the night, the floodgates of memory open, and Nicholas begins to scrawl episodes from his past into a notebook. From these memories – sometimes poignant, sometimes comic, and often involving Philip Larkin – a picture soon emerges: of a devastating first love, and a fragile mind struggling to stay sane in a world that seems headed for annihilation.

Dexter's tragi-comic *tour de force* will be adored by anyone who has ever asked themselves: *am I crazy, or is everyone else*?